FOOTBALL LEGENDS
of All Time

BOB CARROLL

JOE HORRIGAN

PUBLICATIONS INTERNATIONAL, LTD.

Bob Carroll is a prolific author of more than 20 books and over 200 articles about sports history. His credits include *The Hidden Game of Football* (with John Thorn and Pete Palmer) and *Pro Football: When the Grass Was Real*, the story of the game in the 1960s. He also served as an editor for the book *Total Football: The Official Encyclopedia of the National Football League*. In addition to writing, he is a sports artist whose illustrations appear regularly in several national publications.

Joe Horrigan is the vice-president of communications/exhibits at the Pro Football Hall of Fame, where he previously served as the curator/director of research information. He is the author of *The Pro Football Hall of Fame Answer Book* and was a contributing writer for *Total Football: The Official Encyclopedia of the National Football League*. A charter member and past president of the Professional Football Researchers Association, he was the 1991 recipient of that organization's Ralph Hay Award for lifetime achievement in the field of pro football historiography.

Editorial Assistance: James Campbell

OPPOSITE PAGE: *Chicago's Walter Payton rushed for an NFL-record 16,726 yards, 3,467 more than runner-up Eric Dickerson.*

CONTENTS

INTRODUCTION

While thousands of young men have played the game of football, only a relative few can be counted among the sport's elite. They're the men whose names and athletic accomplishments have or surely will survive the test of time. You won't find the "one-year wonder" or the "almost great" in this book. Recounted within these pages are stories of the best the game has offered. *Football Legends of All Time* provides a freeze-framed look at the men who not only made football America's most popular sport, but its passion.

Included are stories of the game's pioneers, such as Amos Alonzo Stagg, Jim Thorpe, and Red Grange. Grange, known as the "Galloping Ghost," epitomized football during the "Golden Age of Sports"—the 1920s. The decision of this electrifying runner from the University of Illinois to turn pro with the Chicago Bears in 1925 was headline news and drew the first pro football sellout to Chicago's Wrigley Field.

Others who followed, such as Bronko Nagurski, kept the romance of the game alive during the Great Depression. His very name inspires images of the bruising style of 1930s football. He was so tough that when one coach was asked how he planned to stop him, he merely shrugged and said, "With a shotgun as he's leaving the locker room."

As the game matured, great passers emerged. It's no exaggeration to say that Sammy Baugh was a major factor in turning football from the grind-it-out days of old into the exciting, air-it-out modern game. While "Slinging Sammy" was putting the ball up, there may never have been a better receiver pulling them down than Green Bay's Don Hutson. His 488 career receptions were 200 more than anyone else had to that point.

Names such as Joe Schmidt, Dick Butkus, Gino Marchetti, and Ray Nitschke—football tough guys of the

QUARTERBACK SAMMY BAUGH AND THE
Washington Redskins battle the Chicago Bears in 1942. These two powers met in the NFL championship game four times from 1937–43, each winning a pair.

1950s and 1960s—are all here. Their "impact" on the game was felt by every ball carrier who ever faced them on the field. They were the game's intimidators.

There are other players who, in addition to their on-the-field greatness, were synonymous with an era or event. Such a man was Joe Namath. Broadway Joe's "guarantee" boast of victory before Super Bowl III can only be compared to Knute Rockne's "win one for the Gipper" when you talk about impact statements in football lore. Namath talked the talk, but he more than walked the walk. Namath, the first pro to pass for more than 4,000 yards in a season, was more than the New York Jets' star; he was the American Football League's hope. Other AFL stars such as the Kansas City Chiefs' Willie Lanier, Buck Buchanan, and Len Dawson are also remembered in this book.

Success, as most people realize, can't be measured in win-loss columns or official game statistics alone. There are the intangibles—those things that so often separate the near-great from the truly great. *Football Legends of All Time* is not just straightforward biographies and statistical reviews. The 100-plus stories go beyond yards gained and passes thrown. Johnny Unitas's rise from the sandlots of semipro football to superstardom, the accidental discovery of Deacon Jones by a pro scout, and Don Maynard's second-chance career with a new league are a few examples of unusual circumstances that affected the careers of some of these great players.

Not forgotten in this book are the special relationships between teammates. Would Deacon Jones have been as effective rushing the quarterback if teammate Merlin Olsen hadn't tied up the middle? Would Joe Montana have racked up his passing records had Jerry Rice not been so reliable?

Important, too, are the stories that show that even men like Vince Lombardi, a true legend, were not perfect. In a moment of self-criticism, Lombardi once reflected on his near-mishandling of all-time great Herb Adderley. "I was too stubborn to switch him to defense until I had to," he said. "Now when I think of what Adderley means to our defense, it scares me to think of how I almost mishandled him."

Football Legends of All Time is an exciting look at the pageantry of autumn. It's a salute to America's greatest warriors—the men of football.

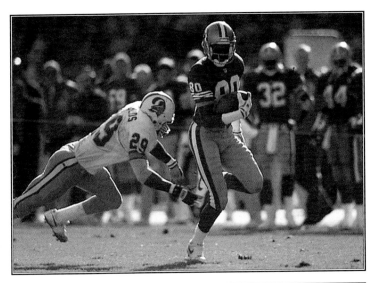

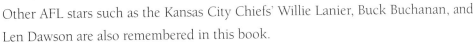
JERRY RICE BECAME THE FIRST NFL *player to surpass 100 touchdown receptions—then smashed the 150 barrier in 1996.*

HERB ADDERLEY

Michigan State, Adderley was chosen to play in the 1961 College All-Star Game. But Packers coach Vince Lombardi knew his future was on defense.
OPPOSITE PAGE: *Adderley added to his five Green Bay championship rings after joining Dallas in 1970. The Cowboys won their first title the next year.*

When Herb Adderley reported to his first Green Bay Packers training camp in 1961, he had the unenviable task of competing against future Hall of Fame running backs Jim Taylor and Paul Hornung for a starter's spot. Hampered by a preseason injury and inexperience, the Michigan State star had to settle for a spot on the special teams unit. Then, on Thanksgiving Day in a game in Detroit, starting cornerback Hank Gremminger was injured. Coach Vince Lombardi decided to insert a by-then healthy Adderley as an emergency replacement. Using his speed and marvelous instincts, Adderley quickly demonstrated that he had what it took to be an NFL cornerback. He even made the first of his 48 career interceptions that day.

Lombardi later admitted that he almost made a mistake with Adderley. "I was too stubborn to switch him to defense until I had to," he said. "Now when I think of what Adderley means to our defense, it scares me to think of how I almost mishandled him."

Adderley (born 1939) went on to play cornerback for nine seasons with the Packers and for three more with the Dallas Cowboys. During that time, he was selected to five consecutive Pro Bowls and was named all-league five times. In addition to outstanding play on defense, Adderley was also a terrific kickoff return specialist, particularly during his years with the Packers. In 1962, he returned a kickoff 103 yards for a touchdown. In 1963, he brought one back 98 yards for another score.

Without doubt, Adderley benefited from the supporting cast of players he had in both Green Bay and Dallas. Six of Herb's defensive teammates—four with the Packers and two with the Cowboys—joined him as members of the Hall of Fame. Proud of his accomplishments, Adderley once remarked, "I always wanted people who watched me play to say when they left the stadium, 'He's the best cornerback I've ever seen.'" Few would argue.

LANCE ALWORTH

Lance Alworth was the "prize catch" of the young American Football League when, in 1962, he signed with the San Diego Chargers instead of the NFL's San Francisco 49ers. Al Davis, then a Chargers assistant coach, signed Alworth. "Lance was one of maybe three players in my lifetime," he said, "who had what I would call 'it.' You could see right away he was going to be special."

Alworth (born 1940) was a much-heralded All-America halfback from the University of Arkansas. A three-year starter, he gained 1,257 yards rushing, caught 38 passes for 666 yards, returned 51 punts for 690 yards, and brought back 31 kickoffs for 740 yards. To say he was versatile would have been an understatement.

He became known as "Bambi" in the pros, a nickname he disliked. Teammate Charlie Flowers gave him the name his first day in training camp. "I looked like a kid of about 15," Alworth explained. "I had real short hair and brown eyes. Charlie said I looked like a deer when I ran." During his nine years with the Chargers, the deer-like receiver averaged more than 50 catches and 1,000 yards per season. An All-AFL choice and an AFL All-Star Game performer seven straight years, Alworth literally filled the AFL record book with his amazing feats.

Lance played for the Chargers through the 1970 season before switching to the Dallas Cowboys for the final two campaigns of his brilliant career. In 11 pro seasons, he caught 542 passes for 10,266 yards and 85 touchdowns. He caught at least one pass in every AFL game he played, including a then-pro-record 96 straight.

Alworth, more than any other player, epitomized the wide-open style of offense featured in the AFL. His patented leaping catches and blazing after-the-catch runs are legendary. It was only fitting that in 1978 he became the first AFL player to be elected to the Pro Football Hall of Fame.

BELOW: THE FIRST TRUE SUPERSTAR OF *the young AFL, Alworth caught at least one pass in every one of the 96 AFL games in which he played.* **OPPOSITE PAGE:** *Alworth was extremely durable. Although a freak injury in his rookie season caused him to miss 10 games, he missed just seven more during the remainder of his nine years in San Diego.*

DOUG ATKINS

O ne day, a rookie offensive guard held Doug Atkins at the line of scrimmage and got away without a flag. A veteran tackle from his team pulled the rookie aside. "I've got to play against him the rest of the day," the tackle yelled. "Now you go apologize!"

For 17 long seasons, from 1953–69, NFL linemen knew to avoid angering Atkins (born 1930). Even when all was right in Atkins's world, he was awesome. At 6'8" and 275 pounds, he could blot out the sun for a quarterback attempting to pass. If a blocker hazarded in front of him, he might leap over him in a single bound or pick him up and throw him at the quarterback. But, if he was angered, he might really get serious.

Doug originally went to the University of Tennessee on a basketball scholarship, but once the football coach saw his combination of size and agility, he was recruited for the grid team. After he earned All-America honors as a defensive tackle, the Cleveland Browns made him their first draft choice in 1953.

An outspoken free spirit, Atkins was not Cleveland coach Paul Brown's kind of player. After two seasons, he was traded to the Chicago Bears, where he clashed with Bears owner-coach George Halas. Once, after some disagreement at practice, Halas told him to run laps and, to make it particularly uncomfortable on a hot day, ordered Doug to wear his helmet. When he looked up, Halas saw Atkins running his laps wearing his helmet—and nothing else! Despite occasional explosions, Halas put up with Atkins for 12 seasons because the big guy was such a defensive force. Atkins, who was All-NFL three times and named to eight Pro Bowls, was a key part of the great Bears defense that won the league championship in 1963.

Finally, in 1967, Atkins was traded to New Orleans, where he finished his career. After Atkins retired, Halas admitted, "There never was a better defensive end."

BELOW: A CONFERENCE HIGH-JUMP *champion and scholarship basketball player at the University of Tennessee, the 6'8" Atkins used his size and speed to wreak havoc on opposing quarterbacks.* **OPPOSITE PAGE:** *Atkins sheds his blocker and zeroes in on Bart Starr. Jim Parker, a Hall of Fame lineman, confessed he considered giving up football in his rookie season after a match-up with Atkins.*

SAMMY BAUGH

ABOVE: SAMMY BAUGH ARRANGES *16 game programs symbolizing his then-record for the most years active as an NFL player. Baugh held 11 other regular-season records when he retired in 1952.* **OPPOSITE PAGE:** *Teammates simulate line play as Baugh performs for the cameras. No one was a more accurate tosser than "Slingin' Sammy."*

According to legend, Washington Redskins coach Ray Flaherty once diagrammed a deep pass play for his team, then remarked to his passer, Sammy Baugh, "When the end cuts way down here, Sam, I want you to hit him in the eye." Baugh, knowing the accuracy of his arm, asked, "Which eye, coach?"

Although this oft-quoted story probably never happened, it indicates the precision of the tall Texan's passing. Until "Slingin' Sammy" Baugh (born 1914) arrived in the NFL after an All-America career at Texas Christian University, no one had ever seen a passer who could throw long, short, and in-between with such fantastic accuracy.

As a rookie in 1937, Baugh led the Redskins to a championship. In 1942, he and the 'Skins took another title. On three other occasions, Baugh's passes took the Redskins to championship games. For all of his 16 seasons, his tosses kept his team exciting and competitive. He led the NFL in passing a record six times. In 1945, he completed 70.3 percent of his passes.

It's no exaggeration to say that Baugh's fabulous success with the pass was a major factor in turning football from the grind-it-out days of old into the exciting, air-dominated modern game. It's no wonder that in 1963 he was named as a charter member of the Pro Football Hall of Fame.

In the mid-1940s, at the height of his career, Baugh was asked to learn a new position. Within a year, he had made a successful transition from a single-wing tailback to a T-formation quarterback, as he led Washington to another division title.

Baugh was such a great passer, it is sometimes forgotten that he did everything well. His 51.4 punting average in 1940 is still the NFL record, as is his career average of 45.1. He was an effective runner when the situation demanded as well as a top pass defender. In 1943, he led the league in passing, punting, and interceptions—a triple crown.

CHUCK BEDNARIK

The Eagles had to beat the Giants. A victory would give Philadelphia a clear road to the 1960 division title; a loss would mean the likelihood of another year as an also-ran. So when Chuck Bednarik slammed into Giants star runner Frank Gifford late in the game, separating him from the football and preserving the Eagles' win, Bednarik did an impromptu victory dance. He didn't know Gifford was still lying unconscious on the ground behind him, but from the stands it looked like he was dancing with glee at Gifford's injury. Gifford went to the hospital—he was out of football for a year—and Giants fans went wild with angry charges of dirty play. Eventually, films showed that Bednarik's tackle was perfectly legal—bone-jarring but legitimate, the kind he had been making for years.

Bednarik (born 1925) didn't really get into football until he returned from World War II (after 30 combat missions over Nazi Germany). He showed up unheralded at the University of Pennsylvania but was a consensus All-American in his last two seasons for the Quakers. The 6′3″, 235-pound star was the Eagles' No. 1 draft choice in 1949, then became a starting center for Philadelphia's NFL champions.

Over the next few years, Bednarik won all-league honors regularly at linebacker. Then, in the late 1950s, he went back to center on offense. After 1959, with 11 seasons under his belt, he was ready to retire, but the Eagles talked him into coming back for what turned out to be the magical 1960 season. Early in the season, when a shortage of linebackers developed, he was asked to go both ways—center on offense, linebacker on defense. At the age of 35, he undertook a grueling task that men 10 years younger couldn't even consider. He was both sensational and inspirational. The Eagles won their division and the league championship. The title game ended appropriately with Bednarik tackling Green Bay's Jim Taylor short of a touchdown and then sitting on him until time ran out.

BELOW: FOR HIS 1960 "IRON MAN" *performance, Bednarik received numerous awards and citations. Here, "Concrete Charlie" graciously accepts yet another, the Sundialer Award.* **OPPOSITE PAGE:** *A World War II B-24 waist gunner and Air Medal recipient, Bednarik frequently thwarted the opposition's air attack with outstanding defensive play, including the occasional interception.*

BOBBY BELL

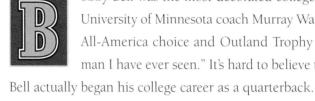

high school before becoming an all-state quarterback. At Minnesota, he first played quarterback but wound up as an All-America tackle. In the pros, he was a defensive end before moving to linebacker. **OPPOSITE PAGE:** *Regularly timed at 4.5 in the 40-yard dash, Bell used his speed and size to contain the opposition. In this 1967 game, Bell lowers the boom on Raiders quarterback Daryle Lamonica.*

Bobby Bell was the most decorated college lineman of the 1962 season. University of Minnesota coach Murray Warmath described the two-time All-America choice and Outland Trophy winner as "the greatest lineman I have ever seen." It's hard to believe the versatile 6'4", 225-pound Bell actually began his college career as a quarterback.

The Kansas City Chiefs of the fledgling American Football League were so convinced that Bell (born 1940) would sign with the rival NFL's Minnesota Vikings that they didn't even bother selecting him until the seventh round of the 1963 draft. The Gophers star stunned the pro football world, however, when he opted to sign with the Chiefs. "I liked the way the club treated me," he offered.

Bell, a tremendously skilled athlete, demonstrated his versatility in the pros by playing defensive end before moving to linebacker. As a defensive end, he excelled in coach Hank Stram's "stack" defense, which called for him to drop out of the 4–3 alignment and become a fourth linebacker. In 1965, after winning all-league honors as a defensive end, Bell was shifted to outside linebacker, where he remained for the rest of his career. His size and 4.5 speed made him ideal for the position. "I just liked to play football," Bell said, "no matter what the position."

Big plays were commonplace for the talented Bell, who won All-AFL or All-AFC designation nine times. In a 1965 game, he recovered two fumbles that were converted into touchdowns in a 14–10 victory over the New York Jets. A year later, he followed a touchdown-saving tackle with an interception that set up a game-winning touchdown over the Boston Patriots. During his 12-year career, he intercepted 26 passes, returning six for touchdowns. He also scored on an onside kick and a fumble recovery.

Teammate Buck Buchanan called Bell "the best all-around football player I ever saw. He's the best defensive end, corner linebacker, and anything else defensively in the whole universe!" Bell earned universal acclaim in 1983 with his election to the Pro Football Hall of Fame.

RAYMOND BERRY

BELOW: A SURE-HANDED RECEIVER, *Berry fumbled only once during his remarkable 13-year career.* **OPPOSITE PAGE:** *For three consecutive seasons, Berry led the NFL in receptions. This 1960 photo illustrates his remarkable leaping ability, soft hands, and ability to concentrate.*

Raymond Berry stumped the panel when he appeared on the TV show *What's My Line?*. How could this slim fellow in glasses be a professional football player? Had they known he needed special shoes because one leg was shorter than the other or that he wore a corset for his bad back, they would have been even more incredulous.

To add to his unlikely story, Berry (born 1933) didn't become a starter for his high school team until his senior year—even though his father was the coach! As an end for Southern Methodist, he caught all of 33 passes in three seasons. What possessed the Baltimore Colts to draft him as a "future" on the 20th round in 1954 is a mystery. And though he managed to stick on the team in 1955, his 13 pass receptions did not suggest he'd be there long.

But Berry was determined. He practiced and practiced, catching passes from anyone willing to throw to him, including his wife. He learned to catch passes thrown over his head or at his feet. He had, at best, average speed, but he developed, by his own count, 88 moves to get open. He ran patterns within a millimeter of how they were drawn up on the blackboard.

In 1956, Johnny Unitas became the Colts' quarterback. By then, Berry was ready to put all those hours of practice to use. He and Unitas emerged as one of the great pitch-and-catch duos in NFL history. In the next 11 seasons, Berry caught over 600 passes, most of them from Unitas. He led the NFL in total receptions three times and retired with the then-record of 631 receptions.

Perhaps his greatest moment came in the overtime 1958 championship game. He caught 12 passes for 178 yards and a touchdown. Several of his grabs came in the Colts' life-or-death, last-minute drive to the tying touchdown. In the overtime period, two Unitas-to-Berry passes good for 33 yards were the major gains in Baltimore's march to the winning score.

MEL BLOUNT

Mel Blount was the prototype cornerback of his era and a major reason why the Pittsburgh Steelers were the dominant team of the NFL in the 1970s. He had ideal size, speed, and quickness, plus the toughness and mental ability to adjust his coverage tactics to rule changes that favored receivers.

The 6′3″, 205-pound Georgia native played his college ball at Southern University. In 1970, Pittsburgh made Blount (born 1948) a third-round draft choice. Although he excelled on the kickoff return team as a rookie, with a 29.7-yard average, it took him a while to become a top cornerback. By 1972, he was ready: He didn't allow a single TD pass all season. In 1975, the year the Steelers won their second Super Bowl, Blount was named the NFL's most valuable defender by the Associated Press. That season, he led the NFL (and set the Steeler record) with 11 pass interceptions.

The Steelers' defense of the 1970s boasted such stars as Joe Greene, Jack Ham, L. C. Greenwood, and Jack Lambert. Blount more than held his own in that glittering company. He was known for his rugged play, making hard but clean tackles all over the field. His specialty was the "bump-and-run" pass defense. He'd stick to a pass receiver, shoving and bumping him down the field. Because of his size and speed, Mel literally overpowered pass catchers.

Midway through Mel's career, NFL rulemakers made such harassment of receivers illegal five yards past the line of scrimmage. They could have called it "The Blount Rule." But even after the rule took away his favorite technique, Blount remained one of the league's best cover men. In 1978 and '79, he helped the Steelers to two more Super Bowl victories.

Blount, who played an even 200 games for the Steelers, finished his 14-season career with a Pittsburgh-record 57 interceptions. He was named All-NFL three times and to the All-AFC team on numerous occasions. He played in five Pro Bowls and, in 1989, was elected to the Pro Football Hall of Fame.

BELOW: BLOUNT HOLDS THE STEELERS' *records for interceptions in a season (11) and a career (57). In one stretch, he intercepted passes in six straight games.* **OPPOSITE PAGE:** *Receivers who caught passes in Blount's territory risked life and limb. Here he man-handles Oakland's Cliff Branch in a 1976 game.*

TERRY BRADSHAW

As an injured Terry Bradshaw was being helped off the field at Three Rivers Stadium, the home crowd of rabid Pittsburgh Steelers rooters booed him. No doubt that was the nadir in a career that witnessed more lows than are normally associated with an acknowledged superstar.

His problem was that superstardom was expected, indeed demanded, by Steelers fans long before it was achieved by the immensely talented young quarterback. Selected by Pittsburgh as the first player chosen in the 1970 draft after a stellar career at Louisiana Tech, he was proclaimed the "franchise quarterback" who would lead the team to its first championship after nearly four decades of frustration. He never lacked the tools. Bradshaw (born 1948) had a rifle arm, size, intelligence, and desire. But in the beginning of his career, he sometimes had too much faith in his arm and forced his passes, resulting in interceptions.

And although he was bright enough, Bradshaw came out of Louisiana Tech with little knowledge of how to read defenses or run a pro offense. Worse, his friendly manner and sly wit were often misconstrued as a lack of "smarts." When a Dallas linebacker joked that Terry "couldn't spell 'cat' if you spotted him a 'c' and a 't,'" fans laughed. Bradshaw was deeply hurt. He struggled through some mediocre seasons before finally coming into his own in 1974.

Once Bradshaw matured as a signal-caller, there was no stopping him. He led the Steelers to Super Bowl victories in January of 1975 and '76 as the masterful director of a run-oriented offense. By the time Pittsburgh won two more titles in 1979 and '80, the offense revolved around his passing. He led the NFL in passing in '78. In Super Bowls XIII and XIV, he was named MVP. Perhaps because he had been through so much, he was always at his best in big games. In postseason play, Bradshaw passed for 3,833 yards and 30 touchdowns.

In his 14 NFL seasons, Bradshaw threw for 27,989 yards and 212 touchdowns. Appropriately, the final pass of his career was for a TD.

BELOW: THOUGH THE FIRST PLAYER *drafted in 1970, success did not come quickly for Bradshaw. By 1972, however, he began a reign in Pittsburgh that resulted in eight divisional titles and four Super Bowl wins.* **OPPOSITE PAGE:** *Bradshaw's career statistics are impressive, but his performances in 19 postseason playoff games were awesome. His 3,833 yards and 30 TDs set NFL playoff records.*

JIM BROWN

BELOW: THE INTROSPECTIVE SUPERSTAR *was far more than a running machine. His best-selling autobiography,* Off My Chest, *published in 1963, revealed his concern for issues larger than winning football games.* **OPPOSITE PAGE:** *Not only a football superstar, Brown was an All-American lacrosse player in high school and the starting center in basketball at Syracuse University. The New York Yankees offered him a baseball contract.*

Every couple of years, when some young turk is tearing up NFL gridirons, someone polls various experts to name "the greatest runner of all time." The consensus is always the same—Jim Brown.

Paul Brown, his coach with Cleveland from 1957–62, said: "As a pure runner, Jim Brown was the best ever. He had a combination of power, intense speed, and a shuffling foot action that made it difficult to stop him. Jim rarely fumbled, and his durability was unusual." In nine NFL seasons, he never missed a game. In 1958, 1963, and 1965, he was named the league's MVP.

After an All-America senior season at Syracuse, Brown (born 1936) was Cleveland's first draft choice in 1957, but only because the quarterback they coveted had already been picked. Brown led the NFL in rushing as a rookie, a feat he would accomplish in all but one of his pro seasons. In seven of his nine seasons, he rushed for over 1,000 yards even though the NFL played only 12-game seasons until 1961. Despite consistently leading all rushers in attempts, he was never seriously injured, not only because of his remarkable durability but also because of his intelligence; he always knew where everyone was on the field and thus knew exactly where a hit was likely to come from.

Eventually, he and coach Brown disagreed over Cleveland's carefully scripted offense. Jim believed the attack had become too predictable. When Blanton Collier replaced Paul Brown as Cleveland coach in 1963, he installed a "run-to-daylight" offense that gave Jim more options. Brown responded with his greatest season—1,863 rushing yards. In 1964, Cleveland won the NFL championship, then followed with a division title the next year.

When Jim retired from football to pursue a movie career before the 1966 season, he held most of the NFL's career and single-season rushing records. Though others with longer careers and 16-game seasons have surpassed his career totals, his lifetime 5.2 average per carry is still the best in NFL history. No other player with more than 1,000 carries has cracked the 5.0 barrier.

PAUL BROWN

with his players after their 21–7 victory over the San Francisco 49ers for the Browns' fourth consecutive AAFC title. **OPPOSITE PAGE:** *Brown, an excellent judge of football talent, must have really liked what he saw in Lin Houston (#32). Brown coached the rugged lineman in high school (Massillon, Ohio), college (Ohio State), and the pros.*

Paul Brown's cool, strict personality put some people off. Away from football, he could be charming, but on the field he was all business. Brown won no congeniality awards, but he won football games everywhere he went.

Brown (1908–1991) was an ordinary player at Miami University in Ohio. His talents were cerebral rather than physical. Hired as an assistant football coach at Severn Prep School in 1930, he helped head coach Bill Hoover compile a 16–1–1 record over two seasons and then returned to his high school alma mater at Massillon, Ohio, where he became a legend. Over nine seasons, his teams went 80–8–2 and won several state championships. In 1941, he became head coach at Ohio State. At first demeaned as only a "high school coach," Brown won the national championship in his second year at Columbus. During World War II, he coached the Great Lakes Naval Training Station to one of the best records among service teams.

Hired as coach of the Cleveland professional team in the newly formed All-America Football Conference, Brown produced an unequaled record of success. The Browns (from a "name-the-team" contest sponsored by a newspaper) won four straight AAFC titles, then entered the NFL in 1950 and won the championship in their first year. In Cleveland's first eight NFL seasons, Brown's club won three league championships and seven division crowns.

Among the many innovations Brown introduced were the scientific study of films, modern pass-blocking techniques, written intelligence tests for players, a "messenger guard" system for sending in plays, and many new passing schemes. Although he had experienced only one losing season, Cleveland owner Art Modell fired him after the 1962 season, stating that the game had passed the coach by.

Five years later, in 1968, Brown came back to pro football as founder and coach of the AFL expansion Cincinnati Bengals. With a roster made up mostly of castoffs and raw recruits, the coach "the game had passed by" won a division title in 1970 and repeated in 1973.

ROOSEVELT BROWN

I n the 1950s, the NFL's annual player draft went 30 rounds. Toward the end of the sessions, teams often found themselves casting around desperately to find names to fill the last few draft slots. When the New York Giants reached the 27th round in 1953, they had no one left on their "wish list." Fortunately, someone in the Giants' front office dimly remembered reading about a big tackle from Morgan State on a Black All-America Team published in the *Pittsburgh Courier*. And thus, Roosevelt Brown became a Giant.

After signing a contract for $2,700, Brown (born 1932) arrived in training camp with a confidence based on his mistaken belief that he couldn't be cut from the squad. Early in camp, Giants coach Steve Owen saw Brown's size (6′3″, 255 pounds) and speed, but Owen also realized the young man was woefully lacking in technique. As a test, he set Brown in a one-on-one drill with New York's All-NFL defensive tackle, Arnie Weinmeister. The result was predictably brutal. But even though Brown took a fearful beating, Owen recognized Brown's potential. Technique, after all, could be taught. Within a few weeks, Brown became a starting offensive tackle for the Giants, a position he held for the rest of his 13-season career.

The Giants won the 1956 NFL championship and added five division titles from 1958–63. Most of the headlines went to the famed "DEE-FENSE" or such offensive stars as Frank Gifford and Chuck Conerly; as usual, the offensive linemen were more or less anonymous to the public. However, close observers recognized the contributions of Brown. He was named All-NFL nine straight years, and he was selected to nine Pro Bowls. When Brown was named to the Pro Football Hall of Fame in 1975, he was the second lineman to achieve that honor on the basis of playing offense only.

BELOW: THE GIANTS DRAFTED BROWN *on the 27th round only after they happened to see his name mentioned in the* Pittsburgh Courier *when he was named to the Black All-America team.* OPPOSITE PAGE: *A loose football is the object of focus for the hard-charging Brown (#79), a heads-up player who earned nine Pro Bowl invitations.*

BEAR BRYANT

Paul Bryant began his college football career as the "other" end to Don Hutson on the University of Alabama's 1935 Rose Bowl team. Hutson went on to become one of pro football's all-time stars, but Bryant, though drafted by the NFL in 1936, opted to become an assistant coach at his alma mater. It was a decision that would eventually lead him to an eminence in college football even greater than what Hutson achieved among the pros.

In 1940, Bryant (1913–1983) took a position as assistant to Henry "Red" Sanders at Vanderbilt, but after two years he left to serve in the Navy during World War II. He received his first chance as a head coach at the University of Maryland in 1945, where he compiled a 6–3–1 record. The following year, he moved on to the University of Kentucky. Over the next eight seasons, he took the Wildcats to a 60–23–5 record and victories in three bowl games. Among the All-America players he developed were quarterback Babe Parilli and tackle Bob Gain. Bryant coached from 1954–57 at Texas A&M, where he developed back John David Crow into a Heisman Trophy winner. His 25–14–2 record included the 1956 SWC championship.

In 1958, he was called to Alabama, which was then in a down cycle. Bryant turned that around and went on to his greatest success. He coached the Crimson Tide for 25 seasons through 1982. His teams won or shared 13 SEC titles and were named national champions six times, in 1961, '64, '65, '73, '78, and '79. Overall, they were 232–46–9 and fielded such stars as Joe Namath and John Hannah. Bryant was named the national Coach of the Year three times, and when he retired, his 323 career victories were the most ever achieved by a college coach up to that time. Only Grambling's Eddie Robinson has since surpassed that mark.

Nicknamed "Bear," Bryant was a large, powerful man with a growling voice and a gruff manner. Although he was a strict disciplinarian, he also earned his players' deep loyalty by taking a concerned interest in their lives.

BELOW: AS A TEENAGER IN ARKANSAS, *young Bryant wrestled a bear at a traveling show, earning him the nickname "Bear."* **OPPOSITE PAGE:** *A victorious Bryant is carried off the field after capturing his 314th career win, tying the legendary Amos Alonzo Stagg.*

BUCK BUCHANAN

Robinson called Buchanan "the finest lineman I have ever seen." **OPPOSITE PAGE:** *Buchanan not only had the speed to chase down backs like the Patriots' Larry Garron, but he also possessed the size and strength to stand them straight up and strip away the ball.*

I thought the opportunities would be better in the AFL," explained Buck Buchanan when asked why he signed with the Kansas City Chiefs before entertaining an offer from the rival NFL. Maybe he was right. The young AFL had, after all, actively recruited players from traditionally overlooked schools like Buchanan's Grambling. Also, the AFL did have the reputation of being an "equal-opportunity" league for African-American players. But in hindsight, there is little doubt that the talented Junious "Buck" Buchanan (born 1940) would have found "opportunity" wherever he chose to play.

"Buck had it all—size, speed, quickness, and great, great attitude," bragged Chiefs coach Hank Stram. "He gave us the big player and the big personality we needed." At 6'7" and 287 pounds, and as fast as he was strong, Buchanan quickly became a dominant force with the Chiefs—and the prototype for future defensive linemen.

Although Buchanan played both end and tackle his rookie season, Stram installed him into his permanent right defensive tackle spot in 1964. Starting that year, he was named to either the AFL All-Star Game or AFC/NFC Pro Bowl eight consecutive times. As Buck's play improved each year, so too did the Kansas City Chiefs teams that won three division championships, two AFL titles, and Super Bowl IV. Throughout, Buchanan was a consistent force who made things happen. In 1968, the Chiefs' defense, led by Buchanan and teammate Bobby Bell, held the opposition to a league-low 170 points.

In Kansas City's 23–7 victory over the Minnesota Vikings in Super Bowl IV, Buchanan was the key man in coach Stram's "triple-stack" defense, which called for Buck to line up over Vikings center Mick Tingelhoff. Buchanan so dominated the All-Pro center that he neutralized a prime Minnesota strength, Tingelhoff's blocking of the middle linebacker. This disrupted the Vikings' normal blocking assignments and gave the Chiefs the edge they needed to win the AFL-NFL championship clash.

DICK BUTKUS

ho's the best at any position is always cause for debate. But when you mention great middle linebackers, Dick Butkus is at or near the top of everyone's list. "When they say All-Pro middle linebacker," the Chicago Bears standout once remarked, "I want them to mean Butkus."

Consumed with the idea of being the best, Butkus (born 1942) admittedly played every game as if it were his last. No one ever played with more intensity. His nine years of outstanding play with the Bears earned him All-Pro recognition seven times as well as eight Pro Bowl invitations. He was even voted by a panel of NFL coaches as the one player they would want to have to start a new franchise.

A two-time All-American at the University of Illinois, Butkus was drafted by the Bears in the NFL as well as by the Denver Broncos of the rival American Football League. Desirous of playing in his hometown of Chicago, he signed with the Bears. From the very start, he was a fan favorite. "The day he reported to training camp," his predecessor at middle linebacker, Hall of Famer Bill George, once reflected, "I knew my days were numbered. There was no way he wasn't going to be great."

Nicknamed the "Maestro of Mayhem," Butkus had the speed and agility to make tackles from sideline to sideline and to cover running backs and tight ends on pass plays. In his first game as a pro, he recorded 11 unassisted tackles. As a rookie, he led the Bears in interceptions and opponents' fumbles recovered. In 1967, team statisticians reported that the one-man wrecking crew was involved in 867 of 880 defensive plays, leading the team with 111 solo tackles, 35 assists, and 18 quarterback sacks.

During his career, Butkus intercepted 22 passes and recovered 25 opponents' fumbles, an NFL record at the time of his retirement in 1973. In 1979, in his first year of eligibility, Butkus was accorded pro football's highest honor, election to the Pro Football Hall of Fame.

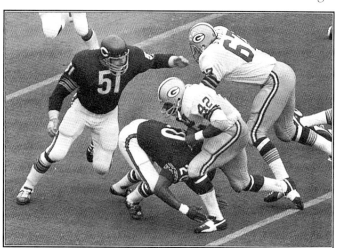

ABOVE: A TERROR ON DEFENSE, *Butkus had a consuming desire to punish ball carriers. A devastating tackler, he recorded 25 fumble recoveries during his career.* **OPPOSITE PAGE:** *Butkus had the speed and agility to cover the best tight ends and running backs on pass plays. His career stats include 22 interceptions.*

EARL CAMPBELL

ABOVE: OILERS COACH BUM PHILLIPS *was so certain Campbell would be great, he designed a new "I-formation" offense for him before he ever played a game for Houston.* **OPPOSITE PAGE:** *Campbell's demeanor was quiet, almost shy, off the field, but when the whistle blew, it was wham, bam, crash, smash!*

Described as a "one-man demolition team," Earl Campbell was a punishing runner. He packed 36-inch thighs on a 5'11", 233-pound frame to make him the most feared running back of his time.

Campbell (born 1955) won the 1977 Heisman Trophy while playing for the University of Texas, leading the nation with 1,744 yards rushing. He was the first player chosen in the 1978 NFL draft. Selected by the Houston Oilers, Campbell blossomed immediately, rushing for a league-best 1,450 yards. It was the first time a rookie led the league in rushing since Jim Brown did it 21 seasons earlier. For his efforts, Campbell was named Rookie of the Year, All-Pro, and the NFL's Most Valuable Player. It was more of the same the next two seasons, with rushing titles, MVP honors, and consensus All-Pro acclaim each year. Pittsburgh Steelers defensive tackle Joe Greene claimed that Campbell could inflict more damage on a team than any back he had ever faced.

Although he rushed for more than 1,000 yards in five of his first six seasons, Campbell's finest season came in 1980, when he rushed for an incredible 1,934 yards, the third-best rushing performance in NFL history. That year, the bruising back rumbled for more than 200 yards in a record four games.

Campbell's most famous single-game performance, however, came in a Monday night game against the Miami Dolphins in his rookie season. That night, in front of a national television audience, he ran for 199 yards and four touchdowns, including a picturesque 81-yard dash late in the game that sealed a 35–30 victory over the Dolphins.

Unfortunately, the constant pounding Campbell absorbed during his eight-year career finally took its toll. In 1985, after a season and a half with the New Orleans Saints, Campbell announced his retirement. Five years later, he was elected to the Pro Football Hall of Fame.

JACK CHRISTIANSEN

In a game against the Los Angeles Rams in 1951, Detroit Lions rookie Jack Christiansen ran back two punts for touchdowns. Later in the season, he did it again against Green Bay to prove it was no fluke. No other NFL punt returner has ever had more than one two-touchdown game in a season. Nor has anyone ever topped the four TD returns he had for the '51 season or the eight he had for his career. His 21.47 average yards per return for 1952 is the second highest ever, as is his 12.75 career average. A case can be made that Christiansen was the greatest punt returner ever.

That said, it can also be added that Christiansen (1928–1986) would have earned his 1970 election to the Pro Football Hall of Fame if he had never returned a single punt. His primary value to the Lions during his eight-year career (1951–58) was as a magnificent defensive back. "He was instrumental in the overall development of our defense," said Detroit coach Buddy Parker. "He ran it and he was the boss."

The Lions' defensive backfield during the period, known quite properly as "Chris's Crew," was one of the most effective ever and contributed mightily to Detroit's three NFL championships and four division titles during Jack's tenure. Christiansen personally contributed 46 interceptions, leading the league in 1953 and 1957.

Christiansen, who was raised in an orphanage, thought he had little chance in football when he entered Colorado A&M. Not only was he a mere 162 pounds, but also a shooting accident had weakened his left arm. As a freshman, he ran track. Coaxed out for football as a sophomore, he was the last player on the team's 44-man traveling squad until an injury to another player raised him to regular status as a standout two-way back.

The Lions drafted Christiansen on the sixth round in 1951 and assigned him to the defensive team. From there, he went on to be named All-Pro six times.

ABOVE: A COACH ON THE FIELD WHEN *he played in Detroit, Christiansen was the San Francisco 49ers' head coach from 1963–67.* **OPPOSITE PAGE:** *As Cleveland Browns receiver Dante Lavelli reaches back with outstretched arms, Christiansen hauls in Otto Graham's aerial attempt. The Lions won this 1954 season ender 14–10.*

WILLIE DAVIS

Bowl I, Davis reflected, "We weren't playing just for the Packers; we were playing for the entire NFL." **OPPOSITE PAGE:** *Davis demonstrates his big-play ability as he swarms L.A. Rams quarterback Roman Gabriel in this 1966 contest.*

A ticket to "Siberia" turned out to be Willie Davis's ticket to stardom. The Cleveland Browns drafted Davis out of Grambling on the 15th round in 1956. He played a couple of years of Army football before joining Cleveland in 1958. For two seasons, he was used sometimes at offensive tackle and sometimes at defensive end, but slowly his playing time increased. He seemed to have a future in Cleveland when suddenly he was traded to the Green Bay Packers in 1960.

Cleveland coach Paul Brown had often threatened his players with a trade to long-time doormat Green Bay, then considered the NFL's Siberia. Davis (born 1934) did not know why he was being punished, but for a time he even considered retiring.

But under coach Vince Lombardi, the Packers were about to experience a renaissance. They had managed their first winning season in over a decade in 1959. Davis decided to report. When he arrived in training camp, coach Lombardi quickly assured him that he had engineered the trade because he needed a top-flight defensive end and he thought Davis could fill the role. "Willie, we have seen some films of you where your reactions are just incredible," Lombardi explained. "We feel with your quickness, you can be a great pass rusher."

Installed as a regular defensive end, Davis was able to use his intelligence, speed, agility, and size (6′3″, 245) to become one of the best in the business. He was All-NFL five times and also chosen for a like number of Pro Bowls. He and Henry Jordan formed the "pass rushing" side of the Packers' outstanding defensive line, while Dave Hanner and Bill Quinlan (later Ron Kostelnik and Lionel Aldridge) concentrated on stopping the run. The Green Bay defense was a major factor in the Packers winning five NFL championships and six division titles in eight seasons. A great team leader, Davis did not miss a single game during his 12-season career.

LEN DAWSON

en Dawson struggled for five frustrating seasons as a backup quarterback for the Pittsburgh Steelers and Cleveland Browns. It was a difficult role for the former Purdue star, who had led the Big Ten in passing three straight years. So in 1962, realizing that his lack of playing time would probably bring a premature end to his hopes for a successful pro football career, he asked to be released from his contract. Browns coach Paul Brown granted his request.

Immediately, Hank Stram, the head coach of the American Football League's Dallas Texans, signed the repressed quarterback, and the rest was history. "I felt Lenny was like sterling silver," Stram said. "He was tarnished but just needed polishing." That year, Dawson (born 1935) led the Texans to their first AFL title, a 20–17 double-overtime victory over the Houston Oilers. For his efforts, he was named All-AFL, played in the AFL All-Star Game, was named the AFL Player of the Year, and won the first of four individual passing titles.

The following year, the Texans became the Kansas City Chiefs, and for the next 13 seasons Dawson was their highly polished quarterback. An extremely accurate passer, the Alliance, Ohio, native led the Chiefs to AFL titles in 1966 and 1969, which led to appearances in Super Bowls I and IV.

While best remembered for his MVP performance in the Chiefs' upset victory over the Minnesota Vikings in Super Bowl IV, Lenny actually had his finest season in 1971. That year, the always poised field general completed 167 passes for 2,504 yards and 15 touchdowns. The Chiefs' hopes for a third Super Bowl appearance ended, however, when they lost the AFC divisional playoff game 27–24 to the Miami Dolphins. The game, which lasted 82 minutes and 40 seconds, was the longest ever played. During his Hall of Fame career, Dawson, who retired in 1975 at 40 years of age, completed 2,136 passes for 28,711 yards and 239 touchdowns.

COOL IN THE POCKET, DAWSON RANKS *among the elite passers of all time with an 82.6 passer rating over 19 pro seasons.*

A SELDOM-USED BACKUP FOR FIVE *seasons in the NFL, Dawson won four individual passing crowns with the AFL's Kansas City Chiefs.*

ERIC DICKERSON

Eric Dickerson was the delivery man for Southern Methodist University's famed "Pony Express" backfield in the early 1980s. The 6'3", 220-pound back gained 4,450 yards in four years at SMU to eclipse the great Earl Campbell's Southwest Conference career rushing record. A No. 1 draft pick of the Los Angeles Rams, Dickerson wasted little time establishing himself as one of the NFL's premier running backs.

In 1983, his inaugural season, Dickerson (born 1960) established rookie records with 390 attempts for 1,808 yards and 18 touchdowns. His Rookie of the Year performance, however, turned out to be just a prelude to an even more amazing sophomore season. That year, Dickerson accomplished the seemingly impossible when he broke O. J. Simpson's single-season rushing record of 2,003 yards set in 1973. By gaining 215 yards against the Houston Oilers in Week 15, Dickerson bested Simpson's record by four yards. The record came on his 27th carry of the afternoon on a play called "47-gap." "We must have run that about 33 times today," Rams head coach John Robinson said after the game. "The blocking was there, the hole was there, and Eric was there." He added 98 yards in the season finale to make the new single-season record 2,105 yards.

Deceivingly fast, Dickerson had an unusual running style. He combined speed, a fluid motion, and power. "Every time Dickerson gets the ball," former New England Patriots head coach Raymond Berry said, "you don't breathe until he's tackled." Dickerson led the Rams to the playoffs in each of his first four seasons and claimed the NFL rushing title three times during the same period. In 1987, after a bitter contract dispute, he was traded to the Indianapolis Colts.

In five seasons with the Colts, Dickerson added three more 1,000-yard seasons for an NFL-record seven consecutive. When Dickerson retired in 1993, the six-time Pro Bowl choice ranked second only to Walter Payton with 13,259 career rushing yards.

BELOW: A POWERFUL RUNNER, *Dickerson averaged an impressive 4.4 yards per carry during his 11-year career.* **OPPOSITE PAGE:** *Stimulated by Dickerson's arrival on Halloween night, the Colts advanced to the 1987 AFC playoffs before losing to Cleveland in a divisional playoff game 38–21.*

MIKE DITKA

ABOVE: AT PITT, THE HARD-NOSED
Ditka played middle linebacker, defensive end, and receiver and was also one of the nation's premier punters.
OPPOSITE PAGE: *A wide-open Ditka catches this Bill Wade pass for a big gain in this 38–17 win over the Los Angeles Rams in 1964.*

Mike Ditka had four teeth loosened in an auto accident just a few days before a game in 1969. His dentist recommended that he not play until they were tightened. Ditka disagreed and instructed his advisor to "pull them." The stunned dentist made a special mouth guard and "Iron Mike" played the next Sunday.

Born in 1939, Ditka was an All-American at the University of Pittsburgh. As a collegian, he was a two-way performer—defensively at end or middle linebacker, and offensively as a tight end. He was also the team's punter. The Chicago Bears drafted him in the first round in 1961. In his rookie season, Ditka caught 56 passes for 1,076 yards and 12 touchdowns. These were impressive numbers for any receiver, but for a tight end they were unprecedented. Ditka was tough, a devastating blocker, and the first tight end to challenge defenses as a downfield receiver.

During his 12 seasons with the Bears (1961–66), Philadelphia Eagles (1967 and 1968), and Dallas Cowboys (1969–72), Ditka recorded 427 receptions for 5,812 yards and 43 touchdowns. The prototype for his position, Ditka was the first tight end elected to the Pro Football Hall of Fame.

The superb play of this five-time Pro Bowl selection often proved to be the difference between winning and losing. This was never more evident than during the Bears' 1963 championship season. In a romp over the Los Angeles Rams, he caught four touchdown passes. A few weeks later, his crushing block freed teammate Ron Bull to score the game's only touchdown in a 10–3 win over Baltimore. Against the Steelers, he turned a short pass into a 63-yard gain to set up a game-tying field goal. In the championship game, he took a third-down 12-yard pass to the 1-yard line. The Bears scored on the next play and went on to win their first title in 17 years. The Bears' next championship victory came 23 years later in Super Bowl XX. Mike Ditka was the head coach.

TONY DORSETT

ABOVE: THOUGH SMALL AT 5'11", 185, *Dorsett possessed great speed and elusiveness.* **OPPOSITE PAGE:** *Hampered by off-season arthroscopic surgery on both ankles and shared backfield duties with Herschel Walker, Dorsett asked to be traded following a disappointing 1987 season.*

In 1977, the Dallas Cowboys surrendered a first-round draft pick and three second-round picks to the Seattle Seahawks just for the right to draft Tony Dorsett. "We've never had a player who demonstrated so much ability in college," remarked pleased Cowboys coach Tom Landry.

Dorsett (born 1954), the 1976 Heisman Trophy winner from the University of Pittsburgh, was a collegiate star of unparalleled proportions. He broke or tied 14 NCAA records and was the first player in history with four 1,000-yard seasons and three 1,500-yard seasons. A four-time All-American, he rushed for an NCAA career-record 6,082 yards and scored 59 touchdowns. His outstanding play led the Panthers to the 1976 national championship with a 12–0 record.

Equally effective as a professional, the 5'11", 184-pound back became the first NFL player ever to gain more than 1,000 yards in each of his first five seasons. He broke the 1,000-yard barrier eight times in nine years, missing only in the strike-shortened 1982 season. The most electrifying runner in Cowboys history, Dorsett was an integral part of the Cowboys' tremendous success during the late 1970s and the 1980s.

Every time the smooth-running Dorsett touched the ball, opponents feared the worst. When Tony rushed for 100 yards in a game, which he did 46 times for the Cowboys, they won 42. He even managed a record 99-yard touchdown run on a broken play in a 1983 contest against the Minnesota Vikings. It happened on a play that called for the Cowboys' other running back, Ron Springs, to get the ball. Misunderstanding the call, Springs left the huddle and returned to the sidelines, leaving the Cowboys with only 10 men on the field. The quick-thinking Dorsett "improvised" and turned the broken play into a record touchdown run.

Dorsett played for the Cowboys for 11 seasons before finishing his brilliant career with the Denver Broncos. During that time, the 1994 Hall of Famer rushed for 12,739 yards, which ranks him third all time behind only Walter Payton and Eric Dickerson.

TURK EDWARDS

In the days of one-platoon football and smaller rosters, a single lineman—particularly one with great size and determination—could dominate a game more than today. On December 6, 1936, with the NFL's Eastern Division championship up for grabs at New York's Polo Grounds, Glen "Turk" Edwards did just that.

Edwards (1907–1973) was the captain and star tackle of the Boston Redskins, who squared off against the three-time Eastern champion Giants that day. Taking matters into his own hands, Edwards blocked a punt, blocked a place kick, recovered two fumbles, made tackles all along the line, and opened gaping holes in the Giants' defense for Boston's backs to scurry through. The Skins won 14–0 and advanced to their first NFL championship game.

Edwards was huge for his time—6'2", 260 pounds—and he used his size and strength to his advantage. But he was also surprisingly agile for a man his size, enabling him to patrol more than his share of the defensive line.

An All-American at Washington State, Turk and his best friend, Mel Hein, helped the Cougars to the 1931 Rose Bowl. When Edwards graduated in 1932, three NFL teams made him offers—Boston, the Giants, and the Portsmouth Spartans. Boston was a new team just starting out, but Edwards liked their offer because it paid best—$150 a game for 10 games. That wasn't bad money during the Depression.

Edwards was named All-NFL in four of his first six seasons. More important, he helped the Redskins move from also-ran status to a division title in 1936 and an NFL championship in 1937, when the team was transplanted to Washington.

Edwards's career ended in bizarre fashion in 1940. As captain, he oversaw the coin toss for another Redskins-Giants game. Then he shook hands with Hein, the Giants' captain, and turned toward the Redskins' bench. Edwards's cleats caught in the turf, his knee buckled, and he never played another down.

BELOW: UPON GRADUATION, EDWARDS *was sought after by three NFL teams— the Boston Braves, the New York Giants, and the Portsmouth Spartans. He went to the Giants, who offered $1,500 for 10 games.* **OPPOSITE PAGE:** *Huge by 1930s standards, Edwards (bottom) was considered one of the most powerful players on either side of the line.*

TOM FEARS

On his birthday more than 45 years ago, Tom Fears caught 18 passes in a single game. No receiver has topped that mark since.

However, if the truth be known, that big day was one of Fears's lesser accomplishments. His team, the Los Angeles Rams, slaughtered the Green Bay Packers 51–14 that day. The 18 grabs were a nice birthday present for Tom, but they were hardly crucial to the game's outcome. The Rams could have won had Tom not played at all.

ALTHOUGH ORIGINALLY PROGRAMMED *by the Rams to play defense, Fears went on to lead the NFL in receptions his first three years as a pro.*

Far more typical of Fears's pass-catching prowess were the three touchdown tosses he caught a week later to lift the Rams over the Bears 24–14 in a playoff for the NFL's Western Division championship. Of even more importance was the final-quarter pass he took from Norm Van Brocklin in 1951 to give the West Coast Rams their first league championship. The play was officially for 73 yards, but 60 of those were Tom's dash to the end zone for the tie-breaking touchdown.

Fears (born 1923) began his college football at Santa Clara, took three years out for military service during World War II, and then finished up with a pair of All-America seasons at UCLA. Ironically, the Rams drafted him with the intention of making him a defensive back. But after he intercepted a couple of passes in his first game, he was installed as a receiver. Fears went on to lead the league in receptions in each of his first three NFL seasons, 1948–50. He improved his total each year, setting a new league record with 77 in 1949 and then smashing his own mark with 84 in 1950.

The 6'2", 215-pound Fears did not possess unusual speed, but he ran extremely precise patterns and was absolutely fearless when catching in a crowd. Although injuries and the emergence of other fine receivers for the Rams limited his number of catches in his final six seasons, he remained a clutch performer in big games.

PHILADELPHIA'S DICK HUMBERT (#81) *makes a last-ditch effort to keep a sprinting Tom Fears from scoring in this 1949 game. Though not fast, Fears ran routes with great precision.*

LEN FORD

BELOW: A SERIOUS FACE INJURY *almost ended Ford's career, but he managed to return and lead the Browns to a dramatic 30–28 victory over the L.A. Rams in the 1950 championship game.* **OPPOSITE PAGE:** *This October 25, 1953, game between the Browns and Giants was a mud-fest, as Ford's and teammate Darrell Palmer's uniforms attest.*

Len Ford's first pro coach said of him: "Len can become the greatest all-around end in history. He has everything—great size, speed, strength, great hands." Although Jim Phelan was right in his assessment of Ford's talents, he was wrong about the "all-around" part. Ford became a defensive star, one of the best in the history of pro football.

After a stellar career at Michigan—he starred on the undefeated 1947 team that slaughtered USC 49–0 in the Rose Bowl—Ford (1926–1972) joined the Los Angeles Dons of the All-America Football Conference. For two seasons, he made Phelan's prediction look inspired. He played both ways, specializing in spectacular one-hand catches and rock-smashing tackles. But when the AAFC merged with the NFL in 1950, the Dons were no more. Len was put into a special draft of players cast adrift by defunct AAFC clubs.

Coach Paul Brown, whose Cleveland team had been taken into the league, grabbed Ford and made him strictly a defender. After some fine games, disaster struck. The Cardinals' Pat Harder, a terrific blocker, caught Len full in the face with an elbow. Ford suffered a broken nose, two fractures of the cheekbone, and several lost teeth. He needed reconstructive facial surgery. It was assumed his season was over. But Len worked hard and was back at defensive end for the championship game. His pass rushing was a factor in Cleveland's narrow 30–28 win.

At 6'5" and 260 pounds, Ford was nearly unstoppable when he went after a passer. An opponent's scouting report described him thus: "LEN FORD: Really blows in. Does a lot of jumping over blockers. Does not predetermine this—if he sees a fellow going very low to block, he will jump over. Plays inside very tough. Must be blocked or he will kill the passer. He claims there is no one in the league who can take him out alone." With Ford an annual All-NFL selection, the Browns played in six straight championship games, winning three.

DAN FORTMANN

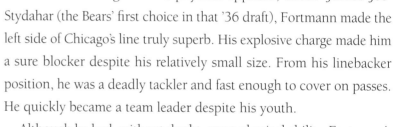

egend has it that canny George Halas chose Colgate guard Dan Fortmann as the Chicago Bears' ninth and last selection in the NFL's 1936 player draft (the first ever held) just because he liked the young man's name. If there's any truth to that, it was certainly a great hunch! In 1965, when Fortmann was named to the Pro Football Hall of Fame, he was only the second guard to be enshrined.

FORTMANN DID NOT TURN 21 UNTIL *after his first season with the Bears. By then, he'd been named second-team All-NFL.*

When Fortmann (1916–1995) joined the Bears in 1936, he was both undersized and underage. Having barely turned 20, the 6′0″, 207-pound "boy" became the youngest starter in the NFL. Along with his physical opposite, tackle "Jumbo Joe" Stydahar (the Bears' first choice in that '36 draft), Fortmann made the left side of Chicago's line truly superb. His explosive charge made him a sure blocker despite his relatively small size. From his linebacker position, he was a deadly tackler and fast enough to cover on passes. He quickly became a team leader despite his youth.

Although he had, without doubt, great physical ability, Fortmann's greatest attribute was his mind. At Colgate, he was a Phi Beta Kappa scholar. With the Bears, he showed his genius by diagnosing enemy plays brilliantly. He earned his medical degree while playing for the Bears, but long before he began practicing medicine, he was an NFL doctor of defense.

Paired with big George Musso, Fortmann gave the Bears the best pair of guards in the league. He earned All-NFL honors six straight years—from 1938 until he retired to enter medicine in 1943. During his eight years with the team, the Bears won three NFL championships and took divisional titles on two other occasions.

Not surprisingly, Fortmann enjoyed continued success in his post-football career as a highly respected doctor on the West Coast. For a time, he was one of the Los Angeles Rams' team physicians.

FORTMANN PLANNED TO BYPASS PRO *football for medical school, but George Halas convinced him he could play for the Bears while attending the University of Chicago Medical School.*

DAN FOUTS

replaced his idol, Johnny Unitas, who earlier that season had become history's first 40,000-yard passer. Thirteen seasons later, Fouts joined Unitas and Fran Tarkenton as just the third quarterback to surpass the 40,000-yard mark. **OPPOSITE PAGE:** *Fouts was a perfect passer. His quick drops, rapid reads, and passes thrown "on rhythm" without any hesitation made him the ideal quarterback for the Chargers' "Air Coryell" offense.*

I f ever there was a player destined to be an NFL quarterback, it had to be Dan Fouts. From an early age, Fouts, a San Francisco native, seemed to be in the right spot at the right time. His father, Bob Fouts, was the play-by-play radio announcer for the hometown 49ers and, as such, pulled a few strings to get his son a job as the team ball boy. After Dan led his St. Ignatius Prep football team to a city championship, he went to the University of Oregon, where they ran a pro-type offense. There, he set school records with 5,995 career passing yards and 37 touchdowns.

The San Diego Chargers made Fouts (born 1951) a third-round draft pick in 1973. As a rookie, he was a backup to his "idol," Johnny Unitas. Fouts replaced the battered veteran in the fourth game of the 1973 season. Dan was never out of the starting lineup again.

Although Fouts's play improved each of his first three seasons, the team did not. Then in 1976, the Chargers named Bill Walsh offensive coordinator, and Fouts's career really began to blossom. His good fortune continued when, in 1978, Don Coryell signed on as the team's new head coach. Coryell implemented a high-powered, pass-oriented offense, and from then on it was "bombs away." Fouts directed the offensive assault dubbed "Air Coryell."

With Fouts at the controls, Air Coryell transformed the Chargers from also-rans to AFC Western Division champs in 1979, 1980, and 1981. Named both NFL and AFC Player of the Year in 1979, he led the conference in passing and broke Joe Namath's record for passing yards gained in a season (4,082). In 1980, Fouts broke his own yardage record with 4,715 yards, then broke it again in 1981 with 4,802. In 1982, he again earned NFL Most Valuable Player honors.

In 15 seasons, Fouts completed 3,297 passes for 43,040 yards. At the time of his induction into the Pro Football Hall of Fame (1993), he was one of only three quarterbacks to pass for more than 40,000 yards.

BILL GEORGE

ill George's football career, with apologies to Neil Armstrong, might be summed up as "one tiny step backward for a middle guard, one giant leap forward for pro football defense."

While no one can swear which middle guard in a five-man line first dropped back to play at middle linebacker and create the classic 4–3 defense, George (1930–1982) gets more votes than anyone else. Certainly he was the first to star at the middle linebacker position.

Coming out of high school, George had mostly wrestling scholarship offers, but he turned them all down for a chance to play football at Wake Forest. He earned some All-America mentions for the Demon Deacons and was drafted in the second round by the Chicago Bears in 1951.

The 6′2″, 230-pound lineman was small for a defensive tackle, so the Bears moved him to middle guard. Coach Clark Shaughnessy summed up George: "He is a rare physical specimen both from the standpoint of power and agility. He's absolutely fearless on the field. He has a brilliant mind, an ability to size up a situation quickly and react to it, and also the ability to retain the complicated details of his job."

It was George's ability to diagnose and react quickly that led the Bears to believe he could move a step backward and become a super middle linebacker—a demanding position requiring sometimes pass rushing and sometimes pass defense, along with sure tackling, the speed to range from sideline to sideline, the agility to avoid blockers coming from all directions, and a sixth sense of knowing what the offense might do next. It was the perfect spot for George.

George was named All-NFL from 1955–61 and again in '63. In 1963, he led the stellar Bears defense that took Chicago to the NFL championship. He was also picked for eight Pro Bowls. In 1972, he was elected to the Pro Football Hall of Fame. "It's a little embarrassing but I'm thrilled to death," he said modestly.

BELOW: WHEN GEORGE DROPPED *back into pass coverage from his middle guard position for the first time, the surprised quarterback's pass hit him right in the stomach.* **OPPOSITE PAGE:** *From his linebacker position, George would occasionally move to his old middle guard position and bull-rush his way toward the quarterback. In this 1963 game, Rams quarterback Roman Gabriel pays the price.*

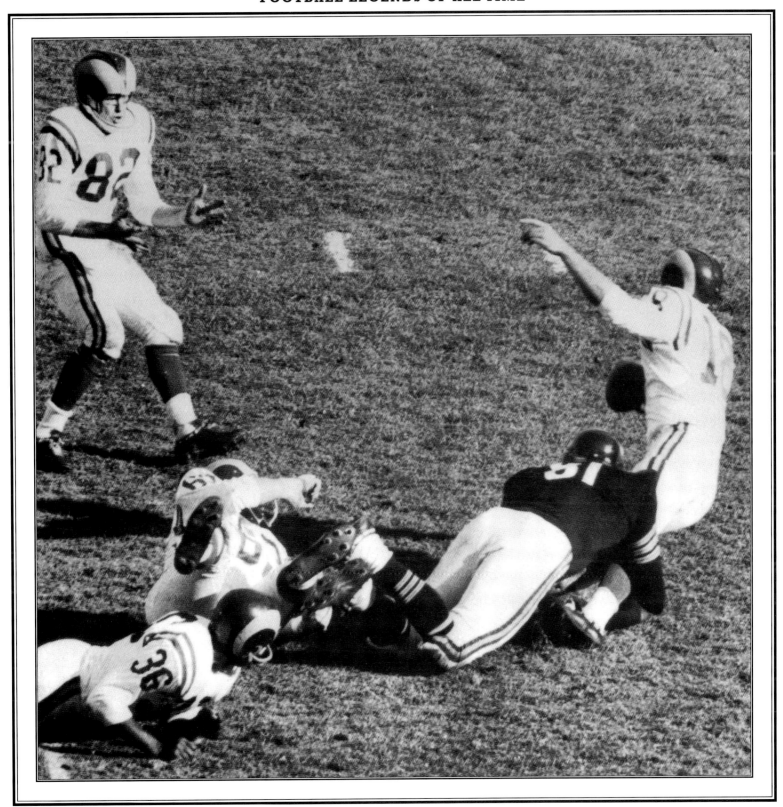

OTTO GRAHAM

BELOW: A COLLEGE BASKETBALL

player at Northwestern, Graham was "discovered" playing intramural football as a freshman. **OPPOSITE PAGE:** *Graham passed for four touchdowns in a 30–28 victory over the Rams in the 1950 NFL championship game (pictured). He found an edge by wearing sneakers on Cleveland Stadium's frozen field.*

Otto Graham retired from pro football in 1955, yet many of his career statistics still rank with those numbers of the top passers of all time. Considering how rule and strategy changes favor more modern passers, Graham's marks are truly remarkable. And yet, if the sign of a great quarterback is not his personal statistics but his ability to win, Otto Graham was the greatest quarterback pro football has ever seen. During his 10 years as trigger man for the Cleveland Browns, Graham led his team to four straight All-America Football Conference titles, six NFL division crowns, and three NFL championships.

Graham (born 1921) had been a fine single-wing tailback at Northwestern University, where he also starred on the basketball court (he even played pro basketball for two seasons). In the 1943 Chicago College All-Star Game, he returned a pass interception 97 yards for a touchdown to seal a victory over the pro champion Redskins.

While at North Carolina Pre-Flight during World War II, Graham was approached by Paul Brown, who was scheduled to coach the Cleveland entry in the AAFC, a new league set to oppose the NFL in 1946. Brown wanted to use Graham as his T-formation quarterback. In their inaugural season, the Browns won their first of four straight AAFC crowns, and Graham proved himself master of his new position.

All-league nine times, Graham was at his best under pressure, accounting for 10 passing touchdowns and five rushing TDs in six NFL championship games. He was sometimes called "Automatic Otto," both as a tribute to his many smooth performances and as a sly dig at Paul Brown's system of calling plays from the sideline years before it was fashionable to do so.

But even the harshest critics couldn't argue with his success. Graham's pinpoint passing, slick ball-handling, and steady leadership kept Cleveland at the top of the standings for 10 straight years "Otto-matically." He was named to the Pro Football Hall of Fame in 1965.

RED GRANGE

barnstorming tour following the 1925 season, more than 400,000 fans saw the fabled "Galloping Ghost" in action. **OPPOSITE PAGE:** *In 1927, Grange suffered a crippling knee injury that kept him out of pro ball until 1929. Although he played for the Bears until 1934, much of his offensive elusiveness was gone.*

Pro football in the 1920s was the "poor relation" of the sports world. That began to change on Thanksgiving Day, 1925, when college football's greatest star, Harold "Red" Grange, took the field in the uniform of the Chicago Bears.

Grange (1903–1991) ranked with Babe Ruth and Jack Dempsey as a giant of the "Golden Age of Sports"—the 1920s. In his first game for the University of Illinois, Grange scored three touchdowns and rushed for 208 yards against Nebraska. Against Michigan, the "Wheaton Iceman" scored four touchdowns in the first 12 minutes on runs of 95, 67, 56, and 44 yards. The modest, 185-pound redhead combined great speed with a mystifying change of pace to score 31 touchdowns in only 20 games for the Illini. Huge crowds flocked to his games in hopes of seeing one of his long, electrifying runs.

Grange's decision to turn pro made headlines all over the country and drew the first pro football sellout to Chicago's Wrigley Field. Ten days later, more than 70,000 paying customers packed New York's Polo Grounds to see Red take on the Giants. Then, the "Galloping Ghost" and the Bears took off on an exhausting tour of the country, winning thousands of new fans for pro football.

Grange and his manager, C. C. "Cash and Carry" Pyle, formed their own pro football league in 1926, with Red's New York Yankees team as the main attraction. Although the "Grange League" folded after one season, Red's personal popularity continued. He made movies, made public appearances, and had many endorsements. The NFL happily took in his orphaned Yankees team for 1927. Unfortunately, a serious leg injury ruined Red's season, kept him out of football for a year, and doomed the Grange-less Yankees. Worse, it cost him much of the elusiveness that had made him football's most feared runner.

In 1929, Grange returned to the Bears. No longer the breakaway threat of old, he remained a clutch performer and a top defensive back for six more seasons. In 1931, when the NFL named its first official All-NFL Team, Grange was selected at halfback.

JOE GREENE

"Joe who?" asked disappointed Pittsburgh fans when the Steelers made the defensive tackle from North Texas State their No. 1 draft pick in 1969. Although the new guy had been a consensus All-American, his reputation hadn't made much of an impression in Pennsylvania. Told he was large (6′4″, 260 pounds) and had a colorful nickname ("Mean Joe"), fans were still unimpressed. They'd wanted a "name" player at a skill position.

Greene (born 1946) became a "big" name in Pittsburgh from his first game. In fact, the lowly Steelers had never had such a dominating lineman. Few, if any, teams ever have. Although the rebuilding Steelers under first-year coach Chuck Noll won only a single game in Greene's rookie year, he was the best lineman on the field in nearly every game.

Big, fast, smart, and determined, Joe was the rock that the Steeler dynasty of the 1970s was built upon. The "Steel Curtain" defensive line of L. C. Greenwood, Dwight

White, Fats Holmes, and Greene became one of the NFL's legendary foursomes. Greene was named Defensive Rookie of the Year in '69, NFL Most Valuable Defensive Player in both 1972 and 1974, and a 10-time Pro Bowler. But his most telling awards were the four Super Bowl rings he and his Steeler cohorts earned during the 1970s.

Ironically, Greene never liked the "Mean Joe" nickname that became so famous, nor could it have been further from the truth—at least off the field. Out of uniform, Joe was a bright, articulate, friendly fellow whom NFL commissioner Pete Rozelle once described as "one of our thinking players." A famous TV commercial in which he gave his game jersey to a young fan who'd shared a soft drink with him was very near the real Joe Greene.

On the other hand, NFL players who only knew Greene from on-the-field meetings had no trouble at all believing his nickname. Some even muttered it in their sleep.

BELOW: DURABLE, GREENE FOUGHT *off injuries through much of his career, playing in 181 of a possible 190 regular-season games.* OPPOSITE PAGE: *Greene was the first defensive tackle to use the tactic of lining up at a sharp angle between the guard and center to disrupt the opposition's blocking assignments.*

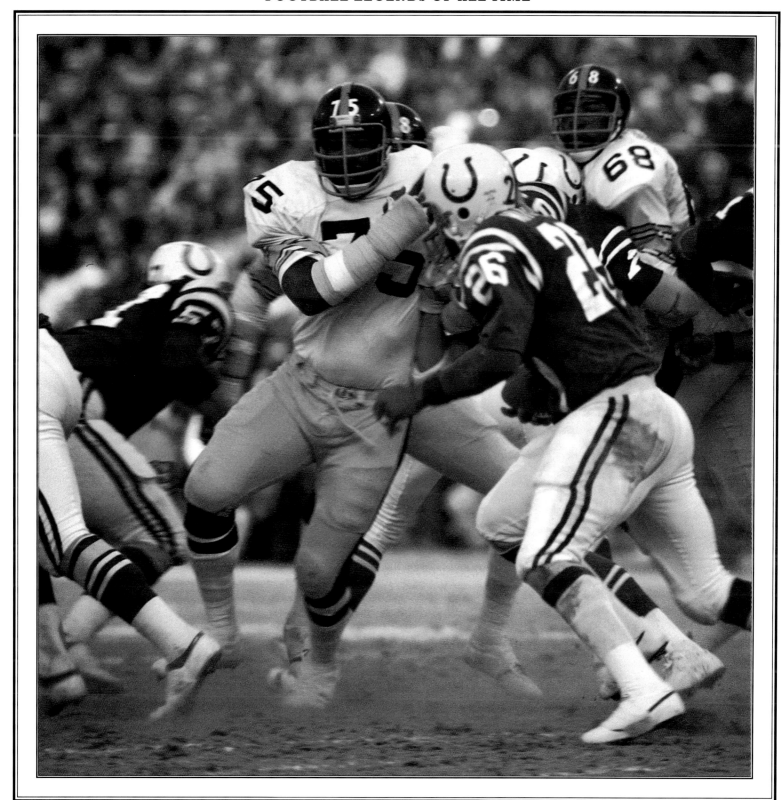

FORREST GREGG

BELOW: GREGG UNSELFISHLY
switched from tackle to guard when injuries created a crisis on the Packers' line. Playing guard here, he serves as the lead block for running back Tom Moore. **OPPOSITE PAGE:** *In this game against the Bears, Gregg tied teammate Jim Ringo's NFL record of playing in 182 consecutive games. Gregg went on to play in 188 straight games.*

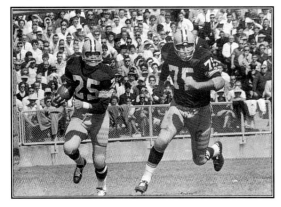

The only thing Hall of Fame tackle Forrest Gregg didn't do well was retire. Four times the Green Bay Packers great tried; three times he was coaxed back. Twice Vince Lombardi talked him into returning. Then in 1971, after Gregg was released by the Packers, Dallas coach Tom Landry convinced him to give it a go one more time. He did, and the Cowboys went on to win Super Bowl VI. Finally, at the age of 38, Gregg retired for good.

Alvis Forrest Gregg (born 1933) was the Packers' second-round selection in the 1956 NFL draft. A two-time All-Southwest Conference player, Gregg played both offensive and defensive tackle at Southern Methodist University. The Packers' coaches, however, assigned the rookie to the offense.

Even at 6'4" and 230 pounds (he matured to 250 later in his career), Gregg was considered small for an offensive lineman. Realizing his size limitations, he concentrated on learning ways to out-finesse the big defensive ends who would be looking to overpower him. He spent countless hours watching films and learning players' weaknesses and tendencies. By the time an opponent lined up against him, Forrest already knew what he had to do to beat him.

During his early years with the Packers, the team struggled. Then in 1959, Lombardi took over the coaching reins and all that changed. As the Packers' fortunes improved, Gregg finally began to get the national recognition he deserved. He won All-NFL honors eight straight times (1960–67) and played in nine Pro Bowls from 1960–69. "Forrest Gregg," Lombardi said, "is the finest player I ever coached!"

Always in peak condition, Gregg played in a then-record 188 consecutive NFL games from 1956–71. A team player, he demonstrated his unselfish versatility in 1961 and again in 1965 when injuries forced him to move to guard. He made the move willingly and with exceptional results. Following the 1965 season, he was named as an all-league tackle by one major news service and an All-NFL guard by another. In 1994, Forrest Gregg was named to the NFL's All-Time Team.

GEORGE HALAS

Today the Pro Football Hall of Fame in Canton, Ohio, sits on George Halas Drive. No address could be more appropriate. Halas is arguably the most important figure in the history of pro football.

At the University of Illinois, Halas (1895–1983) was a good, though not great, two-way end. In 1919, he played pro football in Chicago and, briefly, major-league baseball with the New York Yankees. A hip injury ended his baseball career. A. E. Staley, owner of a Decatur, Illinois, starch company, hired Halas as coach of the company's baseball and football teams.

By offering players positions with the company plus paid practice time, Halas was able to build a strong football team. When he learned a league was to be formed in Canton in 1920, he made the Staleys charter members. In the early years of the NFL, Halas was one of the most steadfast and influential leaders at league meetings.

In 1921, Halas moved the Staleys to Chicago and won his first league championship. The next year, he and partner Dutch Sternaman secured their own franchise and renamed the team the Chicago Bears. Halas raised pro football enormously in the public's estimation in 1925 by signing All-American Red Grange and launching a coast-to-coast barnstorming tour that played to huge crowds.

After a hiatus, Halas returned to coach the Bears in 1933 and won his second NFL title. His greatest period as a coach was the 1940s, when his Bears won four league crowns. Much of that success was due to the development of the modern T-formation pioneered in part by Halas and his assistants. The Bears' dominance led to the "T" becoming the standard football offense.

Halas won his final NFL championship in 1963 with a team keyed by a magnificent defense. In 40 years of coaching, Halas compiled a 324–151–31 mark. Only Don Shula, in an age of longer seasons, has won more pro games. Until his death in 1983, Halas continued to be a leader among NFL owners.

BELOW: HALAS WAS THE ONLY PERSON *to be a part of the NFL from its very beginning in 1920 until 1983, when he died. He served as a league founder, player, coach, general manager, and owner.* OPPOSITE PAGE: *Halas celebrates with his players after their 73–0 thrashing of the Washington Redskins in the 1940 title game. Halas called the one-sided contest "his greatest thrill."*

JACK HAM

Jack Ham began his pro career with a misconception. He thought "you had to be bigger than life." At 6′1″ and 210 pounds when he reported to his first Pittsburgh Steelers training camp, Ham was definitely on the small side for a pro linebacker. "That's why I didn't know how long my career would be," he said.

It turned out to be 12 glory-filled years. Ham (born in nearby Johnstown in 1948) was named All-NFL from 1974–79 and picked for eight consecutive Pro Bowls. The near-perfect outside linebacker for the Steelers' four Super Bowl winners of the 1970s was chosen to the All-Pro squad of the 1970s by the Pro Football Hall of Fame. In 1988, he was enshrined in the Hall.

But back in 1971, Jack, a second-round draft choice out of Penn State, was a none-too-confident rookie. He won a starting slot in his final preseason game with three interceptions against the New York Giants. Throughout his career, the quiet, unassuming Ham showed a penchant for making big plays. When he retired after the 1982 season, Jack had 32 pass interceptions and 19 opponents' fumbles recovered. A sure tackler and excellent pass defender, Ham had such a knack for blocking kicks that for much of his career he continued to play on the Steelers' special teams.

"He was superb," said Andy Russell, who was the other outside linebacker in Ham's early years. "I played the position for 14 years and watched film of every great linebacker you could mention. . . . There was nobody better than Jack. People don't realize it, but in a five-yard dash Jack Ham was the fastest man in pro football. He had incredible acceleration that allowed him to come off a block, retain his balance, and explode. He'd make tackles look routine on plays where the rest of us would try to dive."

Penn State has had so many fine linebackers that it's sometimes called "Linebacker U.," but Ham is the school's valedictorian.

BELOW: HAM CLINCHED THE STEELERS' *starting left linebacker spot following a three-interception performance in the final preseason game of his rookie year. He remained a starter until he retired following the 1982 season.* **OPPOSITE PAGE:** *Ham earned the reputation as a big-play defender. He finished his career with 19 fumble recoveries and 32 interceptions.*

JOHN HANNAH

ABOVE: IN SPITE OF THE CONSTANT *pounding he absorbed as an NFL lineman, Hannah missed only eight games during his 13-year career.* **OPPOSITE PAGE:** *Hannah finished his career in 1985 on a high note, as he earned All-Pro honors and a Pro Bowl invitation while his team won the AFC championship.*

eammates nicknamed John Hannah "Ham Hocks" in college and "Hog" in the pros. Both monikers seem appropriate for Hannah. He weighed in at 11 pounds at birth, seemingly born to play football.

A standout performer at the University of Alabama, Hannah (born 1951) won eight letters in three sports. It was, however, in football that the Canton, Georgia, native was in a class by himself. Coach Bear Bryant once said of his two-time All-America star, "John Hannah is the best offensive lineman I ever coached." The son of Herb Hannah, who played for the New York Giants in 1951, and the brother of Charley, a tackle with the Tampa Bay Buccaneers and Los Angeles Raiders, John had football in his blood.

John was the first-round draft pick of the New England Patriots in 1973 and quickly established himself as one of the premier guards in the league. His adjustment from the straight-ahead blocking style to the drop-back blocking and pulling required of pro guards so impressed the Patriots' coaches that they made him a starter as a rookie. He anchored a Patriots line that in 1978 helped establish an NFL record for most yards gained rushing by a team in a season (3,165). The Pats also led the league in rushing in 1982 and 1983.

At 6′3″, 265 pounds, Hannah was not exactly huge for an offensive lineman, but he played "big." "With his attitude," Patriots coach Ron Erhardt said, "John Hannah could play if he had been five feet two."

Although he battled injuries throughout his career, Hannah missed only eight games out of a possible 190 contests. The NFL Players Association's four-time Offensive Lineman of the Year, "Hog" earned All-Pro honors 10 straight years and was voted to nine Pro Bowls. In 1991, with his father Herb serving as his presenter, John Hannah was enshrined in the Pro Football Hall of Fame.

FRANCO HARRIS

T he argument might be made that Franco Harris was the smartest runner who ever played in the NFL. At a well-tapered 225 pounds, he looked like a typical head-down, pile-driving line-smasher. But, while it was true that when necessary he could get the tough inside yards, that wasn't his usual style. Instead, Harris was a fullback who ran like a scatback. A big scatback.

Many of Harris's best runs came when he would knife off tackle and then cut back against the grain. His speed and agility gave him a step on pursuing defenders; his size allowed him to trample those opponents left in his path.

Harris's brainiest runs came when he was trapped along the sideline. With no hope of escape, he would neatly step out of bounds, much to the disdain of Steelers fans who wanted him to try for a few more meaningless inches. Franco knew, of course, that it was more important to the Pittsburgh cause that he stay healthy for the next play. His style enabled him to play 13 seasons in the NFL even though he ran the ball 2,949 times. His 12,120 rushing yards ranked third all time in NFL history when he retired after the 1984 season.

At Penn State, Franco (born 1950) was considered somewhat of an underachiever. Many considered it a stretch when the Steelers made him their first draft choice in 1972. Although he didn't become a starter until late in the season, he rushed for over 1,000 yards and helped put Pittsburgh in the playoffs. In the final seconds of the team's first playoff game since 1947, he caught the "Immaculate Reception," a shoetop grab of a deflected pass that he turned into a touchdown, to give Pittsburgh the victory.

Before he was done, the dignified, soft-spoken Harris led Pittsburgh to four Super Bowl victories. In Super Bowl IX, he rushed for 158 yards on 34 carries and was named MVP.

BELOW: CONSIDERED SOMEWHAT OF *an underachiever at Penn State, Harris became only the fifth rookie in NFL history to rush for more than 1,000 yards.* **OPPOSITE PAGE:** *In 19 postseason contests, the soft-spoken Harris was the leading rusher 13 times.*

MIKE HAYNES

ABOVE: A MASTER AT MAN-FOR-MAN *coverages, Haynes teamed in Los Angeles with Lester Hayes to form one of the best cornerback tandems in NFL history.* **OPPOSITE PAGE:** *Patriots wide receiver Stanley Morgan is dragged down from behind by Haynes, who as a Patriot was selected to play in the Pro Bowl six times in seven years.*

For the Los Angeles Raiders, their December 2, 1984, game against the Miami Dolphins was critical. A loss would have severely damaged the Raiders' playoff hopes. Analysts made frequent mention of the "pressure" the Raiders team faced. But if Pro Bowl cornerback Mike Haynes was feeling the pressure, it didn't show.

On the Dolphins' first possession, Haynes intercepted a Dan Marino pass and returned it 97 yards for a 7–0 lead. Later, Haynes grabbed another and returned it 54 yards to set up another touchdown. The Raiders coasted to a 45–34 victory. For Mike Haynes, it was just another day at the office.

Haynes (born 1953) was a two-time All-American at Arizona State before being drafted by the New England Patriots in the first round of the 1976 NFL draft. He was a Pro Bowl player six of his first seven seasons with the Patriots. During that time, he intercepted 28 passes and was widely recognized as the best cornerback in the league.

Rarely beaten on a deep route, Haynes combined great speed with agility. Opposing quarterbacks realized that the best way to handle Mike was to avoid throwing in his direction. The Patriots also utilized him as a punt returner. In his rookie season, he returned two punts for touchdowns with runs of 89 and 62 yards.

A contract squabble with New England caused Haynes to sit out the first 11 games of the 1983 season before being traded to the Raiders for a first-round and a second-round draft pick. His impact with the Raiders was immediate. A master of man-to-man coverages, he became the final piece of the Raiders' championship-season puzzle. In Super Bowl XVIII, he frustrated Washington Redskins quarterback Joe Theismann with his tight coverages and demonstrated his big-play ability by intercepting one pass and defensing another.

In seven seasons as a Raider, Haynes earned three more Pro Bowl bids and added 18 more interceptions for a career mark of 46. He made the NFL's 75th Anniversary All-Time Team in 1994 and was elected to the Hall of Fame in 1997.

MEL HEIN

enter Mel Hein earned All-America honors at Washington State in 1930, but pro football wasn't interested. When time passed and no team contacted him, Hein took the initiative and wrote to four NFL teams to say he was available. At last, he received a modest offer from the Providence Steam Roller. Reluctantly, Mel signed the contract and dropped it in the mail. A few hours later, Ray Flaherty, an assistant coach with the New York Giants, showed up at his doorstep with a better offer—$150 a game. Hein and Flaherty raced off to the post office, where a friendly postmaster helped him retrieve his Providence letter. Then Mel signed with New York.

Neither Hein nor the Giants ever regretted the deal. When the Pro Football Hall of Fame opened in 1963, Hein (1909–1992) was the first center to be enshrined. Hein was quite possibly the best two-way center ever to play pro football. On offense he blocked like a demon, and his faultless centering allowed the Giants to run from a tricky formation in which the ball could be snapped to any one of three men in the backfield. On defense, he was known for his bone-crushing tackles and his ability to cover pass receivers. On top of all that, he was a team leader.

During his 15 years with the Giants (1931–45), the team won seven Eastern Division championships and two league titles. For eight straight years, from 1933–40, Mel was named the center on the All-NFL Team. In 1938, he was selected the NFL's Most Valuable Player, an incredible honor for an interior lineman. During a key late-season win over Green Bay, he intercepted a Packer pass and raced 50 yards to score the only touchdown of his pro career.

Hein's durability was fantastic. In over 200 regular-season, championship, and exhibition games—usually going the full 60 minutes—he never missed a game. Supposedly, he only once needed a time out—for a broken nose.

ABOVE: AN ALL-AMERICA CHOICE

from Washington State, Hein is joined here by end Red Badgro (left) of Southern Cal and tackle Bill Morgan of Oregon. Hein was the best center of his day and the first to be inducted into the Pro Football Hall of Fame. **OPPOSITE PAGE:** *Hein, who purportedly called time out just once during his career (when he needed to fix his broken nose!), wore this early version of a facemask to protect his sensitive snout.*

TED HENDRICKS

BELOW: HENDRICKS SPECIALIZED IN *blocking punts, field goals, and extra point attempts. The "Mad Stork" scored three touchdowns, one on an interception, another on a fumble recovery, and a third on a blocked punt.* **OPPOSITE PAGE:** *Tall and comparatively skinny, Hendricks proved to be not only a punishing tackler, but the kind of player that could totally disrupt an offense. In 15 seasons, he recovered 16 fumbles and intercepted 26 passes.*

Questions abounded when it came time for the pro scouts to rank University of Miami standout Ted Hendricks. He was a three-time All-American who played defensive end and tight end, so what was the concern? Well, he was 6'7", and personnel directors argued that he was too tall and gangly to play linebacker. At 215 pounds, the scouts said, he was too thin to play defensive end. Nonetheless, the Baltimore Colts decided to take the risk and drafted the "Mad Stork" in the second round of the 1969 NFL draft. It turned out to be an excellent move.

Hendricks, born in 1947 in Guatemala City, Guatemala, went on to have a brilliant career with the Colts (1969–73), Packers (1974), and Raiders (1975–83). "Maybe I wasn't the prototype," he explained, "but once I got the experience of playing, then I knew I could play in the big league."

A tenacious player, Hendricks was deceptively strong and fast. And he was a devastating tackler. During his 15-season career, he intercepted 26 passes, blocked 25 field goals or point-after attempts, recorded four safeties, scored 26 points, and earned All-Pro or All-AFC honors eight times. Seemingly impervious to pain, he played in 215 straight regular-season games, eight Pro Bowls, seven AFC championship contests, and four Super Bowls (January 1971 with the Colts and January 1977, 1981, and 1984 with the Raiders).

Surprisingly, the Colts traded Hendricks to the Packers after his five productive seasons in Baltimore. The bigger surprise came, however, when the Packers allowed Ted to play out his option and join the Raiders after just one and possibly his finest season. That year, he had five pick-offs, blocked seven kicks, and scored a safety.

The Raiders, recognizing his unique skills, allowed Hendricks the rare freedom to freelance. Ted simply positioned himself along the line where he thought the play would go, then reacted. He was right so often that the coaches rarely challenged his decision. Ted played nine seasons with the Raiders before retiring in 1983. He was voted to the Hall of Fame in 1991.

CLARKE HINKLE

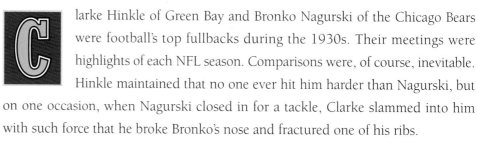

BELOW: HINKLE WAS A TRUE TRIPLE- *threat star in the Packers' backfield. Not only was he one of the game's greatest runners, but he could throw the ball, punt, and place kick.* **OPPOSITE PAGE:** *"Hinkle was the greatest all-around fullback ever to play in the National Football League," said Packers coach Curly Lambeau.*

Clarke Hinkle of Green Bay and Bronko Nagurski of the Chicago Bears were football's top fullbacks during the 1930s. Their meetings were highlights of each NFL season. Comparisons were, of course, inevitable. Hinkle maintained that no one ever hit him harder than Nagurski, but on one occasion, when Nagurski closed in for a tackle, Clarke slammed into him with such force that he broke Bronko's nose and fractured one of his ribs.

Not even Hinkle, who was 30 pounds lighter, could consistently match Nagurski's brutal raw power. But Clarke was more versatile. He not only shattered lines with his power running, but he could also run outside, pass effectively, catch even better, block like a demon, place kick long field goals, punt for distance, back up a line with the best of them, and defend against passes. He insisted that during his career, only one receiver ever got behind him. He was named all-league four times.

Hinkle (1909–1988) starred at Bucknell University and led the East in scoring as a sophomore. In one game, he scored 50 points. After winning All-America honors in 1930 and 1931, he received offers from several pro teams. In those predraft days, a player could sign with any team he chose. The New York Giants were interested and wooed him with an all-expense-paid weekend in New York. The climax was the Giants' Sunday game. Unfortunately, their opponent was Green Bay. When the Packers won impressively, Hinkle decided his future was in Wisconsin.

Hinkle used his football talents to the utmost, playing with a burning desire to win. During his 10 years with the Packers, he helped them win three division titles and two NFL championships, in 1936 and 1939. When he retired after the 1941 season to enter the Coast Guard, Hinkle was the leading rusher in NFL history, with 3,860 yards. He also scored 370 points on 44 touchdowns, 28 extra points, and 26 field goals—and punted for a 43.4 average.

ELROY HIRSCH

ABOVE: ALTHOUGH MITZI GAYNOR *definitely had better looking legs, few if any receivers had better looking over-the-head receptions than did Hirsch. In 1951, "Crazylegs" established a single-season reception record of 1,495 yards gained.* **OPPOSITE PAGE:** *Hirsch won All-America honors at Wisconsin in 1942 and Michigan in 1943. At Michigan, he lettered in four sports— football, basketball, baseball, and track.*

In 1951, Los Angeles Rams receiver Elroy Hirsch enjoyed perhaps the greatest season of any pass catcher in history. Although modern receivers have surpassed his totals—66 catches, 1,495 yards gained, and 17 touchdowns—Hirsch put up those numbers in a 12-game season.

But it wasn't his totals that really set the 6′2″, 190-pound speedster apart; it was how he got them. In that monumental season, he became the most devastating long-distance touchdown threat the NFL had ever seen. Ten of his touchdowns came on long bombs. He scored on touchdown catches of 34, 44, 47, 53, 70, 72, 76, 79, and 81 yards. His longest play came against the Chicago Bears in a must-win game for the Rams. Trailing 14–0 and backed up against their own goal line, the Rams called on Hirsch. He simply outran the Bears' defensive backs, took quarterback Bob Waterfield's pass in stride, and continued on his way to a back-breaking 91-yard touchdown. The Rams beat the reeling Bears 42–17, an important step on their way to the 1951 NFL championship.

Ironically, Hirsch (born 1923) had been considered a disappointment in his first years as a pro. An All-America halfback at both Wisconsin and Michigan, he earned the nickname "Crazylegs" for his unique running style. In 1946, he joined the Chicago Rockets of the newly formed All-America Football Conference. The young league hoped to challenge the established NFL with new stars such as Hirsch. But for three years, injuries ruined his seasons, the worst being a life-threatening fractured skull. When he signed with the Rams in 1949, he was thought by some to be washed up.

In 1950, Rams coach Joe Stydahar shifted Hirsch to end, and, after one season learning his new position, he exploded as a superstar. Even Hollywood jumped on his bandwagon, casting him as himself in the biopic *Crazylegs*. He handled acting well enough to be given the lead in the nonfootball film *Unchained*, best known for its haunting theme song "Unchained Melody." Hirsch retired after the 1957 season with 387 receptions for 7,029 yards and 60 touchdowns.

KEN HOUSTON

ixteen seconds remained in the Monday night matchup between the Washington Redskins and their arch rivals, the Dallas Cowboys. Dallas trailed 14–7 and faced a fourth-and-goal situation. Cowboys quarterback Craig Morton took the snap from center and immediately tossed a short pass to fullback Walt Garrison. Garrison gathered the ball in and turned toward the end zone. All that stood between him and the tying touchdown was Redskins safety Ken Houston. Houston stuffed him. It was perhaps the defining play of Houston's great but, to that point, strangely unnoticed career.

Houston (born 1944) played linebacker at Prairie View A&M before being taken in the ninth round of the 1967 AFL–NFL draft by the Houston Oilers. Undersized (6′3″, 198 pounds) for a linebacker, Houston was wisely converted by the Oilers to a safety. The talented, hard-hitting Houston earned a starter's role by the third game of his rookie season. Two weeks later, in a game against the New York Jets, he scored two touchdowns, one on a 71-yard blocked field goal attempt and the other on a 43-yard interception return.

In all, Ken played six seasons of outstanding football in Houston. During that time, he earned five AFL All-Star Game or Pro Bowl berths. His nine interception returns for touchdowns were an NFL record. Still, outside the AFC Central, he inexplicably remained "Ken Who?".

Then in 1973, Redskins coach George Allen traded five players to the Oilers to secure Houston's services. Many felt Allen paid too high a price. However, after his now-famous fourth game as a Redskin, when he stopped Garrison just inches short of the goal line, Houston made the trade seem like a steal. Never again would he be unnoticed or underrated. Over the next eight seasons, Houston earned All-NFC or All-Pro honors seven times and was selected to play in 10 Pro Bowls.

Altogether, the sensational safety stole 49 passes for 898 yards, recovered 19 opponents' fumbles, and scored 12 touchdowns. Elected to the Pro Football Hall of Fame in 1986, Houston is no longer pro football's unsung superstar.

ABOVE: HOUSTON WAS THE PREMIER *strong safety of his era. With the Oilers, he set an NFL record by returning nine interceptions for touchdowns.*
OPPOSITE PAGE: *In a reversal of roles, Jets wide receiver Don Maynard is forced to play defense as Houston hauls in an errant pass attempt in this 1969 contest.*

CAL HUBBARD

B y the standards of the 1920s, when he first appeared on the pro football scene, the 6'5", 250-pound Cal Hubbard was huge. Moreover, he could run 100 yards in a speedy 11 seconds. The total effect was awesome.

Hubbard (1900–1977) played college football at Centenary and Geneva, hardly the big time. But, when he turned pro in 1927 at the comparatively ripe age of 26, he went straight for the biggest arena of all—New York. The Giants were well stocked at tackle, so Hubbard moved over to become the biggest, most fearsome offensive end in the NFL. On defense, he played linebacker.

The addition of big Cal made a good Giant defense great. The New Yorkers posted 10 shutouts in 13 games and allowed only 20 points for the season while winning their first NFL title. When complacency, age, and dissension dropped the Giants to the middle of the standings the next season, Hubbard asked to be traded.

Hubbard couldn't have timed it better. Cal was sent to Green Bay just as the Packers were becoming a dynasty. He became the key tackle on a team that won NFL championships for three straight years—1929, 1930, and 1931. For all his spectacular defensive play, Hubbard may have been most valuable for his blocking. With his size and speed, he opened holes in the most determined defenses. When the NFL named its first official All-League team in 1931, he was chosen at tackle. In 1932 and 1933, he was named again.

During summers at Green Bay, Cal began umpiring baseball games. In 1936, he began a new career as an American League umpire. He wore the blue for 15 years and then served as supervisor of AL umpires for 15 more. In 1976, the year before his death, he was named to the Baseball Hall of Fame. He was the first person to be enshrined in both the Baseball and Pro Football Halls of Fame.

BELOW: THREE TEAMS OFFERED *Hubbard pro contracts, but his college coach, Bo McMillan, advised him to sign with the New York Giants, who had offered the big lineman the handsome sum of $150 per game.* **OPPOSITE PAGE:** *Hubbard displays his baseball umpiring skills on the gridiron in a photo from 1936, his last year as a player and first as an American League umpire.*

DON HUTSON

Green Bay's tailback faded back to pass as Don Hutson sprinted toward the end zone. Four Chicago Bears guarded Hutson as they neared the big "H" goal posts then set on the goal line. They all crossed the goal line on the dead run, but Hutson's arm shot out and hooked the upright. His body twisted and suddenly he was trotting by himself, in a direction 90 degrees from his previous path. The four Bears were still scrambling to stop their momentum as the Packer passer lobbed a touchdown to a wide-open Hutson.

Hutson (born 1913) invented modern pass receiving. Other ends ran straight to a spot and then waited. He created Z-outs, button-hooks, hook-and-gos, and a whole catalog of moves and fakes. If the throw was poor, he often made an "impossible" catch, because he practiced catching off-target tosses. Once the ball was safely cradled, Hutson's speed and dodging wizardry made him a good bet to score. Then he'd often kick the extra point. From the moment he arrived in Green Bay in 1935, after making All-American at the University of Alabama, Hutson was the NFL's premier receiver.

In one quarter of a 1944 game, he caught four TD passes and kicked five PATs for 29 points. The Packers won three NFL championships—1936, 1939, and 1944—during the "Hutson Era." He led the NFL in receiving in eight of his 11 seasons and in scoring five times. Twice, in 1941 and 1942, he was named the league's Most Valuable Player. Longer seasons and more pass-oriented offenses have helped many modern receivers surpass Hutson's career marks, but when he retired after the 1945 season, his 488 receptions were 200 more than anyone else had. He set an NFL career record with 99 touchdown catches, still a sensational mark.

Hutson played in the backfield on defense for much of his career, intercepting 30 passes during his last six years in Green Bay. In 1963, Don was named a charter member of the Pro Football Hall of Fame.

BELOW: FRESH OUT OF ALABAMA, *Hutson signed contracts with both Green Bay and baseball's Brooklyn Dodgers. Both contracts arrived at the league offices the same day, but Green Bay's had the earlier postmark.* **OPPOSITE PAGE:** *Hours of practice catching "bad" passes paid off when Hutson made amazing receptions in games.*

DEACON JONES

ABOVE: **JONES NOT ONLY COINED THE**
term "sack," he invented his own nickname, figuring "Deacon" would get more attention than plain "David." **OPPOSITE PAGE:** *Jones and Merlin Olsen (#74) gang up on the Chargers' Mike Garrett to cause a fumble in a 1971 preseason game.*

David "Deacon" Jones was an obscure 14th-round draft pick of the Los Angeles Rams in 1961. Flamboyant by nature, he dubbed himself Deacon "because nobody would ever remember a player named David Jones."

"Deacon" wouldn't be the only nickname Jones would invent. He also coined the term "sack," now used to describe the tackling of a quarterback behind the line of scrimmage—something Deacon did extremely well and often during his 14-year career with the Rams (1961–71), San Diego Chargers (1972–73), and Washington Redskins (1974). In 1967, for instance, Rams quarterbacks were sacked 25 times all year, but Deacon by himself dropped opposing quarterbacks 26 times.

An all-conference tackle at South Carolina State in 1958, Jones (born 1938) did not play football in 1959 and transferred to Mississippi Vocational in 1960. Rams scouts, reviewing film of a defensive back prospect from the Mississippi school, noticed this "huge guy" (6'5", 260 pounds) catch a tackle-eligible pass and outrun the defensive back. It was Deacon. The scouts rejected the defensive back and instead drafted Jones. A raw but talented rookie, Deacon was converted to defensive end in training camp.

For 10 seasons (1962–71), Jones and teammate Merlin Olsen combined to give the Rams a devastatingly effective left side for its famous "Fearsome Foursome" defensive front. "You can't believe Deacon's quickness and speed, even when you're playing next to him," said Olsen.

According to Deacon, however, his patented "head slap" was his biggest personal influence on the game. The technique, since ruled illegal, allowed a pass rusher to smash an opposing lineman on the side of his helmet. "You haven't lived until you've had your bell rung by Deacon a few times," groaned Hall of Fame tackle Ron Mix.

Considered by many the best defensive end ever, Deacon was twice named the NFL's outstanding defensive player, selected to play in eight Pro Bowls, named All-NFL or All-NFC six times, and elected to the Pro Football Hall of Fame.

SONNY JURGENSEN

JURGENSEN'S PINPOINT PASSES HELPED *put two of his favorite receivers, Bobby Mitchell and Charley Taylor, in the Pro Football Hall of Fame.*

Quarterback Sonny Jurgensen dissected defenses with his pinpoint passing for 18 seasons, from 1957–74. The fun-loving redhead was a fan favorite. "I had as much fun playing as anybody," he said. "But on the field, it was serious business. I was interested in winning."

A substitute with the Philadelphia Eagles from 1957–60, Jurgensen (born 1934) became a starter in 1961. He promptly led the Eagles to a 10–4 season, winning All-NFL honors, setting two league records, tying a third league mark, and breaking four Eagles marks. His 235 completions, 3,723 yards passing, and 32 touchdown passes were all tops in the NFL.

After two more seasons with the struggling Eagles, Jurgensen was traded to the Redskins before the 1964 campaign. For the next five seasons, he and teammates Bobby Mitchell and Charley Taylor provided an air attack unlike any seen in the nation's capital since Sammy Baugh in the 1930s and 1940s. Still, the best the team could do was post a .500 finish in 1966.

A classic drop-back passer, Jurgensen was known for his poise under pressure. "All I ask of my blockers is four seconds," he said. "I beat people by throwing, not running." In 1969, Vince Lombardi took over the Redskins' coaching reins. Many wondered if the taskmaster coach and the free-spirited quarterback could work together. The answer was a resounding yes. In fact, the two developed a mutual admiration for each other. "In five days, I learned more from him than I had in 12 years of pro football," Jurgensen said.

Under Lombardi, the 1969 Redskins finished second in their division, and Sonny won a second league passing championship. In 1970, Jurgensen had another successful season, completing 22 touchdown passes, but Lombardi's untimely death slowed the Redskins' progress. A series of injuries, coupled with the defensively oriented philosophy of new coach George Allen, limited Jurgensen's playing time over the next few years. Finally, following the 1974 season, Jurgensen—one of the finest pure passers ever—called it quits.

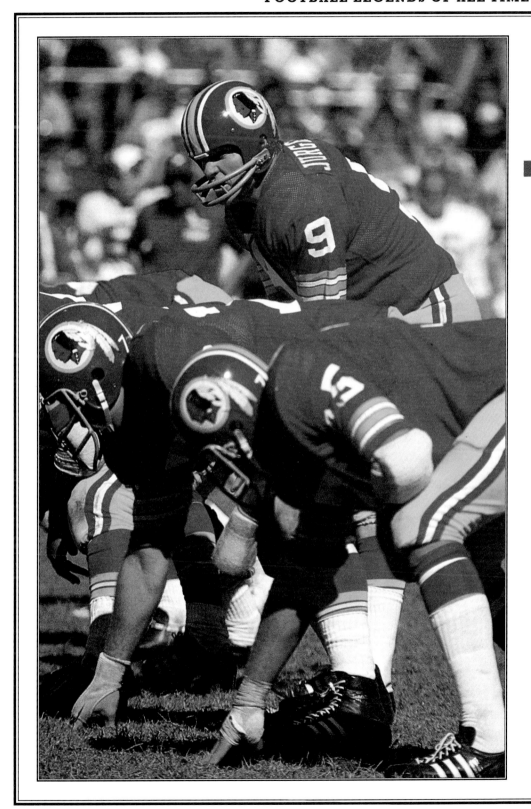

JURGENSEN BARKS OUT HIS SIGNALS.
The affable quarterback was a fun-lover off the field, but he was all business once the game started.

JACK LAMBERT

J ack Lambert played without his front teeth dental bridge, leaving a gap from eye tooth to eye tooth. The effect was to give him the appearance of having fangs. One commentator aptly combined his appearance and playing style in the description "Dracula in shoulder pads."

Lambert (born 1952) was a two-time all-conference defensive end at Kent State and a second-round selection of the Steelers in 1974. The 6′4″, 220-pound blond won the starting middle linebacker assignment in training camp as a rookie and kept the job throughout his 11-year tenure in Pittsburgh. Even though he was the youngest starter on the Pittsburgh defensive unit, many felt that Lambert's presence was the final element needed to turn that unit into a juggernaut.

Lambert had all the necessary ingredients to close down opposing running backs—intelligence, intensity, speed, quickness, range, and durability. He led the Steelers in tackles every year from 1974–83 with a technique that could be described euphemistically as enthusiastically aggressive. Additionally, his height made him a formidable obstacle to passers when they tried to throw over the middle. He intercepted 28 passes in his career and also had 15 fumble recoveries.

Named the NFL Defensive Player of the Year in 1976, Jack was named All-Pro seven times in a nine-year span from 1975–83. He played in nine straight Pro Bowls and was the AFC Defensive Player of the Year in 1976 and 1979. The Steelers' captain for eight years, he played in six AFC championship games and led his team to victory in four Super Bowls.

Lambert enjoyed an uncompromisingly macho image. When rules were passed to try to protect passers from being injured by sackers, it was Lambert who quipped that perhaps quarterbacks should start wearing dresses. Ironically, the injury that ended his football career seemed wimpish to some fans—turf toe. But in truth, his 1984 toe injury made it impossible for him to move with any quickness or agility and was just as decimating as any knee injury.

BELOW: LAMBERT HAD THE MOST *famous two front teeth in football— because he played without them. The result gave him that terrifying "Dracula look."* **OPPOSITE PAGE:** *Lambert calls for a change in the Steeler defense against the Eagles. His height, 6′4″, made him particularly effective in stopping over-the-middle passes.*

TOM LANDRY

F or the first 29 years of their existence, the Dallas Cowboys had only one head coach, Tom Landry. During that time, he delivered 13 division championships, five NFC titles, and Super Bowl victories in January of 1972 and 1978. Landry's Cowboys, dubbed "America's Team," also played in the 1971, 1976, and 1979 Super Bowls.

The always-stoic Landry began his coaching career as a player-coach with the New York Giants in 1954 and 1955. A former University of Texas standout, Landry (born 1924) became a Giants full-time defensive assistant in 1956. By the time he became the head coach of the expansion Cowboys four years later, he was already widely recognized as one of the sharpest young coaches in the game.

As expected, it took a few years before the Cowboys experienced a winning season. But once they did, it seemed they'd never again falter. Under Landry, the Cowboys posted 20 consecutive winning seasons from 1966–85. "That's probably the single most amazing accomplishment of his career," said former Cowboys general manager Tex Schramm.

Landry's coaching career was full of amazing accomplishments. He perfected the "flex defense," a variation of the basic 4–3 alignment, which he used while an assistant coach. Later, when teams copied his system, he simply came up with multiple offense schemes to attack the very defenses he developed.

THE COACH TALKS WITH HIS STAR
quarterback, Roger Staubach, in 1971. Two months later, they'd win the Cowboys' first Super Bowl.

In the 1970s, the innovative coach borrowed a page from the San Francisco 49ers' play book of the early 1960s and gave new life to the "shotgun" formation. Roger Staubach, the Cowboys' shotgun trigger man, flourished under the system. In the 1980s, Landry embraced and helped develop the "situation substitution" concept of inserting players on certain downs for specific assignments.

Landry's coaching career came to an abrupt end early in 1989, when a new Cowboys owner decided to bring in his own coach. Even then, Landry showed his class when he said, "There's always life after football." He compiled a 270–178–6 lifetime record, and he was elected to the Pro Football Hall of Fame in 1990.

THE NATTILY DRESSED LANDRY PACES *the sideline. In his mind, he's already a half-dozen plays ahead of the game on the field.*

DICK LANE

Dick "Night Train" Lane, wrote author Mickey Herskowitz, "was the midnight gambler who never hesitated to take the big risk, who so often made the big play and the key interception. He had superb reflexes and what he modestly described as a 'sense of recovery.'"

Like Emlen Tunnell, another great defensive back, Lane (born 1928) walked into the offices of an NFL team—in Lane's case, the Los Angeles Rams, the reigning NFL champions—in 1952 and asked for a tryout. But, unlike Tunnell, he could not point to experience in college football. He had played a little in junior college, a little in the service. In truth, the young man fresh out of the Army was simply looking for a job—any job—and the Rams were just another door to knock on.

For reasons best known to himself, Rams coach Joe Stydahar agreed to take him to training camp as a receiver. All he had to do was beat out Tom Fears and Elroy Hirsch. When he had trouble learning the plays, Lane went to Fears for counseling. It seemed that every time he showed up at Fears's room, the Buddy Morrow record "Night Train" was playing on the phonograph. "Night Train" became Lane's official nickname.

Soon Lane was switched to cornerback, where he became a surprise sensation. Opponents, figuring the rookie for a soft touch, kept throwing into his territory, and Night Train kept making them pay. The rookie set the all-time interception record with 14 in a 12-game season, and no one has topped that number in a 16-game schedule.

Lane played two years for the Rams and six for the Cardinals before going to Detroit in 1960. Six of his best seasons were with the Lions. Over 14 years, he intercepted 68 passes.

Although he was an exceptional cover man, Lane was even better known for his rough handling of ball carriers and receivers. "Train" was an artist of the blind-side smash, the clothesline maneuver, the neck-high tackle, and the facemask grapple. Interceptions were only one reason to avoid his turf.

BELOW: IN A 1969 POLL OF SPORTS-
writers, Lane was selected the best cornerback in NFL history. **OPPOSITE PAGE:** *Lane applies a typical bull-dogging tackle to Ram Jon Arnett in a 1961 game. Gentleness was never part of Lane's game.*

WILLIE LANIER

His teammates called him "Bear" or "Honeybear," because he looked like a big, friendly teddy bear. Willie Lanier, however, was more like a grizzly when it came time to chase down the opposition. He went after ball carriers ferociously, and he defined the middle linebacker position for 11 seasons with the Kansas City Chiefs.

While his hard-hitting style of play earned him instant recognition as a pro, it came with a price tag. In the seventh game of his rookie season, Lanier (born 1945) suffered a severe concussion after a violent collision with a Denver Broncos ball carrier. "I was not only afraid my career might be over," he said, "but even worse, that my life might not be normal again." Fortunately, Willie was able to return to action after missing just four games. From then on, he wore a specially padded helmet and adopted a "careful" approach to his play.

His new approach must have worked, as he missed only one game in the next 10 seasons while accumulating numerous honors. He was All-Pro, All-AFL, or All-AFC every year from 1968–75, and he was selected to the AFL All-Star Game or the Pro Bowl eight times.

One of Lanier's best-remembered defensive stands came in a 1969 AFL playoff game against the New York Jets. The Chiefs were clinging to a 6–3 lead when the Jets got a first down on the Kansas City 1-yard line. Three times the Jets challenged Lanier and three times they failed. The Chiefs went on to win 13–6 and advanced to Super Bowl IV, where they upset the Minnesota Vikings 23–7.

Many have suggested that no one—not even the fabled Dick Butkus—ever played the middle linebacker position better. Ermal Allen of the Dallas Cowboys' research and development department once remarked, "You hear a lot about Dick Butkus and Tommy Nobis, but this Willie Lanier is really the best middle linebacker in pro football."

BELOW: LANIER WAS THE FIRST
African American to star at middle linebacker, the "glamour position" of the 4–3 defense. **OPPOSITE PAGE:** *Lanier's hard tackle of the Rams' Jim Bertelsen forced a fumble that Kansas City recovered in this 1973 game.*

STEVE LARGENT

When he retired from pro football, Steve Largent held six major pass-receiving records: career pass receptions (819), 50 or more receptions in a season (10), consecutive games with at least one catch (177), yards on pass receptions (13,089), seasons with 1,000 or more yards on receptions (eight), and career touchdown receptions (100). All this by a receiver who the Houston Oilers thought was too small and slow to make it in the pros.

An All-Missouri Valley Conference wide receiver at the University of Tulsa, Largent (born 1954) was selected almost as an afterthought by the Oilers in the fourth round of the 1976 draft. He caught only two passes before being cut following the Oilers' fourth preseason game. "I cried all the way from Houston to Oklahoma City," Largent admitted. "I thought football was over for me."

Instead it was just beginning. Seattle Seahawks assistant coach Jerry Rhome, who had been on the Tulsa coaching staff, recommended Largent to head coach Jack Patera. The expansion Seahawks gave the Oilers an eighth-round draft pick for the castoff receiver. It was the catch of the century for the Seahawks.

ABOVE: LARGENT ZEROES IN ON A PASS *in 1986. Others were faster, some trickier, but no one had surer hands.* **OPPOSITE PAGE:** *Touchdown! Largent leaves a Chargers defensive back grasping air as he increases his TD total on the way to 100.*

Largent became an almost instant star with the Seahawks with 54 receptions, third best in the NFC, in his rookie season. In eight of the nine seasons from 1978–86—every year except the strike-shortened season in 1982—Largent had 66 or more receptions. He had 70 or more catches six times. He led the NFL in receiving in 1979 and 1985.

A possession receiver with just average speed, Largent quickly became known for his precise routes, sure hands, determination, and concentration. His complete mind and body coordination allowed his body to talk, lie, cheat, and steal on the best defensive backs in football. "Running routes became a science to me," Largent said. An NFL Man of the Year winner (1988), Largent was elected to the Pro Football Hall of Fame in 1995.

DANTE LAVELLI

ABOVE: LAVELLI SHOWS AN AMAZED
Otto Graham how he caught one in the Browns' 1946 championship game. Despite the staged photo, Graham wasn't really surprised; he'd seen Lavelli's magic all season. **OPPOSITE PAGE:** *Lavelli demonstrates why he was called "Gluefingers," racing past Steeler Richie McCabe and stretching far out for an "impossible" touchdown.*

Dante Lavelli was called "Gluefingers" for his uncanny ability to hang onto a football, but it wasn't adhesive that fastened him to the Hall of Fame. His hands were not sticky but strong. Cleveland coach Paul Brown said Lavelli had the strongest hands of any receiver he'd ever seen. Those hands helped him be one of the great clutch receivers in pro football history.

Nevertheless, the odds seemed stacked against the 6'0", 199-pound Lavelli (born 1923) when he arrived at the first Cleveland Browns training camp in 1946. Coach Brown had assembled a strong squad for the team's first year in the newly formed All-America Football Conference. Lavelli had played only three games as a sophomore at Ohio State before entering military service, and there were four experienced receivers ahead of him. But they didn't have his hands.

Lavelli not only opened the season as a starting end for the Browns, but he went on to be named All-AAFC in his first two seasons. He ran precise patterns, making him a perfect match for quarterback Otto Graham's pinpoint passing. But, if a play broke down, Lavelli was also adept at improvising to get open.

During his first seven years, Lavelli and Mac Speedie gave Cleveland perhaps the best pair of receivers any team had ever enjoyed to that point. Speedie was the more spectacular of the two and received more honors than Lavelli. But after Speedie defected to Canada, Gluefingers earned new appreciation. He was twice All-NFL and started three Pro Bowls.

Over 11 seasons, Lavelli caught 386 passes, and he was always at his best in big games. In 1950, when the Browns joined the NFL, they were matched in their opening game against the NFL champion Philadelphia Eagles. Experts predicted the upstart Browns would be no match for the champs. Instead, Lavelli and Speedie destroyed the Eagles with button-hook passes as Cleveland won 35–10. That December, in the Browns' championship-game victory over Los Angeles, Lavelli caught 11 passes and scored two touchdowns.

BOB LILLY

Bob Lilly's entire football career, except for his senior year in high school when his family moved to Oregon, was played within a 150-mile radius. He played high school football in the west Texas town of Throckmorton, played college ball in Fort Worth at Texas Christian University, and suited up professionally with the Dallas Cowboys.

An All-America tackle in 1960, Lilly was called by TCU coach Abe Martin "the best tackle I ever coached." In 1961, Lilly became the first-ever draft pick of the Cowboys. Together, Lilly helped the young Cowboys organization mature into one of the most successful sports franchises ever.

Although Lilly (born 1939) spent the majority of his playing days as a defensive tackle, he actually began his career in the pros as a defensive end. He even made the Pro Bowl at that position. However, Cowboys head coach Tom Landry felt that with Bob's astonishing quickness, strength, and agility, he was more suited for the defensive tackle spot. So, in 1963, he made the switch. Lilly made the adjustment with ease and quickly became the main man in Dallas's vaunted "Doomsday Defense."

Nicknamed "Mr. Cowboy," Lilly missed just one game during his 14-year career. During that time, the 6'5", 260-pound lineman earned a Texas-size list of honors. The NFL Rookie of the Year in 1961, he was an All-NFL or All-NFC choice eight times and was selected to play in 11 Pro Bowls. "A man like this comes along once in a generation," the usually reserved Landry said of Lilly. "I don't think Bob ever was aware of how good a player he was or how valuable he was to his team."

It's been said that Lilly was a microcosm of the Cowboys franchise. They struggled together, matured together, and eventually reached the top together with a victory in Super Bowl VI. Lilly even entered the Super Bowl record book that day when he sacked quarterback Bob Griese for a 29-yard loss. Bob Lilly was the first Dallas player elected to the Hall of Fame.

MR. TITTLE, MEET MR. LILLY. THIS *1963 get-together no doubt caused Giants quarterback Y. A. Tittle to consider another line of work.*

VINCE LOMBARDI

Vince Lombardi never said, "Winning isn't everything; it's the only thing." Although that is the quote most often attributed to him, his actual words were: "Winning is not everything, but making the effort to win is." All his life, Lombardi made that effort.

The Brooklyn-born Lombardi (1913–1970) first entered the football limelight during the mid-1930s as a guard on Fordham University's famous "Seven Blocks of Granite" line. He didn't play in the NFL but went directly into coaching. He built a sterling reputation as an assistant with several strong college teams and, in the 1950s, as the New York Giants' offensive coach under Jim Lee Howell.

Meanwhile, desperation had set in with the Green Bay Packers, who were at the lowest point in their history. In 1958, they managed to win only one game. Lombardi was hired as head coach and given complete control. It was the first time he'd been head man other than of a high school team. Lombardi traded for such young players with potential as Willie Davis, changed quarterback flop Paul Hornung into a star running back, nurtured unheralded Bart Starr into a brilliant quarterback, and drove the team mercilessly. Lombardi emphasized execution, blocking, and tackling rather than razzle-dazzle. Most important, he instilled in his players a willingness to "make the effort."

The results were instantaneous. His 1959 team won seven of 12 games. In 1960, Green Bay took its division title, but that was only the beginning. Lombardi's Packers were NFL champions in 1961 and 1962. After two years of retooling, they won titles in 1965, 1966, and 1967. The latter two teams won the first two Super Bowls.

In 1969, the Washington Redskins, another team with a long losing habit, hired Lombardi to turn them around. He was well on his way to doing just that when he was fatally stricken with cancer before the 1970 season. He was named to the Pro Football Hall of Fame in 1971. He is memorialized by the Lombardi Trophy, awarded to each year's Super Bowl winner.

BELOW: THE PACK IS BACK—AGAIN!
Lombardi signals triumph as Green Bay clinches the NFL's Western Conference title in 1966. **OPPOSITE PAGE:** *The Packers hoist their coach after their 1961 championship game win over the Giants—Green Bay's first title since 1944.*

RONNIE LOTT

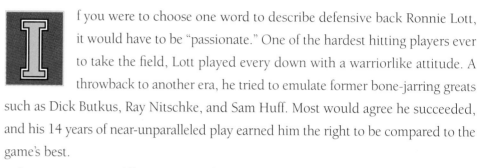

BELOW: LOTT JOINED THE RAIDERS IN *1991. The 49ers had thought he was too old, so he went out and led the league in interceptions for his new team.*
OPPOSITE PAGE: *Here's just one of a lot of Lott interceptions. As a rookie in 1981, Lott turned three interceptions into touchdowns.*

I f you were to choose one word to describe defensive back Ronnie Lott, it would have to be "passionate." One of the hardest hitting players ever to take the field, Lott played every down with a warriorlike attitude. A throwback to another era, he tried to emulate former bone-jarring greats such as Dick Butkus, Ray Nitschke, and Sam Huff. Most would agree he succeeded, and his 14 years of near-unparalleled play earned him the right to be compared to the game's best.

Lott, a consensus All-American in his junior and senior seasons at the University of Southern California, registered 250 tackles during his four-year collegiate career. The Trojans' 1980 MVP, he led the Pac-10 with eight interceptions his senior season.

As a result, the San Francisco 49ers made him their No. 1 choice in the 1981 NFL draft. He went on to become the defensive cornerstone of four Super Bowl champions.

Lott (born 1959) was the complete package. He had speed, strength, and a knowledge of the game that set him apart from most other defensive backs. His accomplishments as a pro are remarkable. During his career with the 49ers (1981–90), Los Angeles Raiders (1991–92), and the New York Jets (1993–94), he twice led the league in interceptions. He ranks fifth on the all-time interception list with 63 steals. He surpassed the 1,000 career tackle mark in 1993, and he had four seasons of at least 100 tackles. The versatile defensive back earned 10 Pro Bowl invitations at three different positions—cornerback, free safety, and strong safety.

A student of the game, Lott had the uncanny ability of being able to sense the direction a play was about to take and then somehow disrupt it. "To break a play down," he said, "you have to see it in slow motion." However he saw it, Ronnie Lott played hard, played clean, and played with passion.

SID LUCKMAN

id Luckman presided over the most lopsided contest in NFL history—the Chicago Bears' 73–0 massacre of the Washington Redskins in the 1940 championship game. It was an historic occasion because it showed just how lethal the Bears' new T-formation could be. The "T" was an ancient formation, but the Bears added men in motion, flankers, new blocking schemes, and numerous deceptive tricks to make it new. In the wake of that game, most teams scurried to copy the Bears' "T." Unfortunately for them, they did not have a Luckman to play quarterback.

Luckman (born 1916) had been a fine triple-threat single-wing tailback at Columbia. Chicago coach George Halas, though, believed Luckman had just the combination of skills as well as the mind to run the intricate new formation the Bears were developing. When he joined the Bears in 1939 and Halas handed him his play book, Luckman was shocked. There were literally hundreds of plays, and each had several variations. As quarterback, Luckman handled the ball on each down. He had to know where every player was on every play as well as which play to call to take advantage of the defense. No player before had been given such a daunting mental task.

It took Luckman the better part of two seasons, but eventually he was able to amaze his coaches with his encyclopedic knowledge of the offense. Everything came together in that fabled championship game. Certainly, Luckman's field generalship was a key to the four NFL titles and five division championships the Bears won in the 1940s. But his lethal long passes also contributed heavily to Chicago's success.

In 1943, when Luckman was voted the league's Most Valuable Player, he had his greatest single game, appropriately enough on "Sid Luckman Day" at New York's Polo Grounds. Sid baffled the Giants for 433 yards and seven touchdowns in a 56–7 slaughter. He was nearly as effective in the championship game that year, throwing five touchdowns against the Redskins as the Bears wrapped up their third title in four years.

BELOW: LUCKMAN WAS GIVEN A
T-formation playbook by Bears coach George Halas (left) even before reporting to training camp. Though initially unsuccessful, Sid developed into the first great "T" quarterback.
OPPOSITE PAGE: *During Luckman's 12-year career with the Bears, Chicago won four NFL championships, including a 73–0 win over the Washington Redskins in 1940.*

JOHN MACKEY

When discussing the play of tight end John Mackey, a Baltimore Colts assistant coach remarked: "Once he catches the ball, the great adventure begins. Those people on defense climb all over him. The lucky ones fall off."

Actually, the "great adventure" began at Syracuse University, where Mackey (born 1941) played halfback as a freshman and sophomore and tight end as a junior. In his senior season, he rushed, caught passes, returned punts, and even intercepted a pass. He scored on explosions of 36, 51, 59, and 40 yards on runs from scrimmage, passes, and punt returns.

Baltimore head coach Don Shula, after selecting Mackey in the second round of the draft, named him the Colts' starting tight end. The 6'2", 217-pound speedster responded with a superb rookie season, catching 35 passes for 726 yards and a career-high 20.7-yard average. He was the only first-year player selected to participate in that year's Pro Bowl.

Mackey was not like other tight ends of his day, who were typically thought of as just another tackle on the line of scrimmage. John added another dimension to the position. His breakaway speed made him a legitimate long-distance threat. In 1966, for instance, six of his nine touchdown receptions came on plays of 51, 57, 64, 79, 83, and 89 yards. His most famous big-play reception, however, came in Super Bowl V when he snared a deflected Johnny Unitas pass and turned it into a 75-yard touchdown completion.

ON THIS PLAY ON SEPTEMBER 18,
1966, Mackey was on the receiving end of Johnny Unitas's then-record 213th career touchdown pass. In Super Bowl V, Mackey turned a deflected Unitas pass into a 75-yard touchdown completion.

A powerful runner, Mackey also had the strength to toss aside would-be tacklers like bothersome gnats. As one veteran Baltimore sportswriter put it, Mackey was his "own best blocker." In 10 seasons with the Colts (1963–71) and San Diego Chargers (1972), Mackey caught 331 passes for 5,236 yards and 38 touchdowns. For three straight years (1966–68), he was the NFL's all-league tight end. In 1992, he became just the second tight end ever to be elected to the Pro Football Hall of Fame.

LIONS DEFENSIVE BACK TOMMY
Vaughn zeroes in on Mackey after he makes one of his 331 career receptions. Mackey's speed and tackle-breaking ability made him the premier tight end of his day.

GINO MARCHETTI

G ino, whatever you do, stay out of the other boys' way so they no hurt you," Gino Marchetti's father warned when reluctantly allowing his son to go out for high school football. Although his boy made the varsity, the elder Marchetti refused to go to any games, certain he'd see his son maimed.

Even when Gino—grown to ample size and a World War II veteran—starred for nearby University of San Francisco, Mr. Marchetti stayed home. When Gino (born 1927) became an All-Pro defensive end with Baltimore, his father avoided games on TV.

IT WAS NOT UNCOMMON FOR TEAMS TO
double- or even triple-team the 6′4″ Marchetti. A perennial Pro Bowl choice, Marchetti was named to the NFL's 75th Anniversary All-Time Team.

He finally consented to tune in when the Colts met the New York Giants for the NFL championship in 1958. He saw his son play brilliantly and lead the desperate rush that stopped the Giants as they tried to ice a victory. The Colts then kicked a tying field goal and went on to win in the first sudden-death overtime. But the senior Marchetti saw something else. On the crucial play, a teammate fell across Gino's leg and broke it in two places. As Gino watched the deadlocking field goal from a stretcher on the sideline, he might well have reflected on his father's advice.

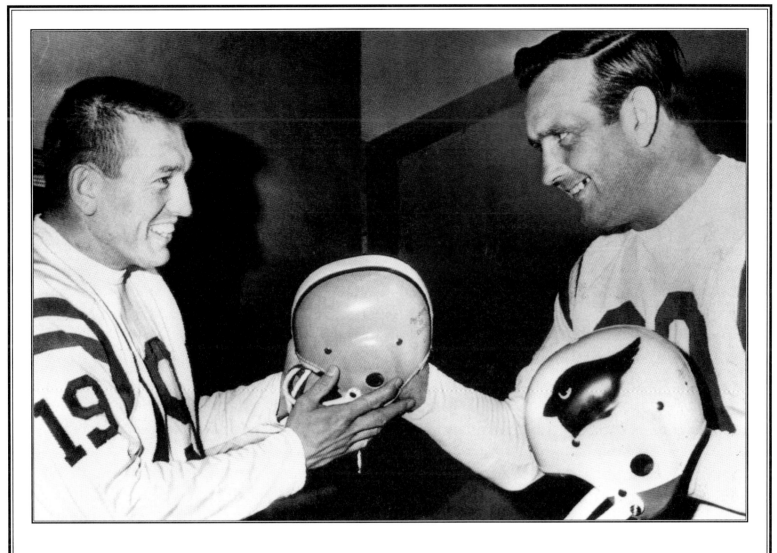

During most of his career, of course, the "other boys" had to stay out of Gino's way. No one played defensive end better. Possessing unusual speed for so large a man, he was deadly against runs and a brilliant pass rusher. Curiously, the Dallas Texans tried to make him an offensive tackle when he joined them as a rookie in 1952. With the reorganized Baltimore Colts in 1953, he found his true niche, crashing past offensive tackles instead of trying to be one.

Veteran coach Sid Gillman called Marchetti "the most valuable man ever to play his position." He was voted All-Pro seven times and played in 10 Pro Bowls (the broken leg kept him out of an 11th). In 1969, he was selected as the best defensive end in the NFL's first 50 years.

MARCHETTI, SPORTING A SINISTER

smile, clowns around with teammate Johnny Unitas in this 1964 photo. Mackey called it quits following the '64 season only to return for one final go-around in 1966.

DAN MARINO

I n 1995, Dan Marino virtually rewrote the NFL's record book for passing. The Miami Dolphins quarterback eclipsed Hall of Famer Fran Tarkenton's career marks in attempts, completions, yards, and touchdowns, making Marino the most prolific passer in NFL history. Not since the great Don Hutson has any player so dominated the NFL career record book.

Marino's quick, accurate release is the nightmare of opposing defensive backs. "He doesn't bring the ball up and throw it with that long arm motion," said Dolphins head coach Don Shula. "It's 'boom' and the ball's gone with a tremendous whip of the shoulders."

Marino (born 1961) entered the NFL in 1983 after four record-setting seasons at the University of Pittsburgh. He was the Dolphins' first-round pick in that year's draft, often called the "Year of the Quarterback," and the sixth quarterback taken, after John Elway, Todd Blackledge, Jim Kelly, Tony Eason, and Ken O'Brien. Marino led the AFC in passing as a rookie and was named the starting QB in the Pro Bowl.

In 1984, in perhaps the greatest season of passing anyone has ever had, Marino ripped the opposition, completing 362 passes for an NFL-record 5,084 yards and 48 touchdowns, also an NFL record. On the strength of Marino's arm, the Dolphins won the AFC title and advanced to Super Bowl XIX, where he set records for attempts (50) and completions (29).

A fierce competitor, Marino's fourth-quarter comebacks are legendary. Over the course of his long career, he brought his team back from a fourth-quarter deficit more than 30 times. In 1993, however, he faced the greatest comeback challenge of his career.

In a midseason game against the Browns that year, Marino went down with a torn Achilles tendon. It was a season-ending if not career-ending injury. But in typical Marino fashion, he returned to action in 1994. He led the AFC in both passing efficiency and touchdown passes that season and was named the Comeback Player of the Year.

BELOW: THE MOST PROLIFIC PASSER IN NFL history, Marino also excelled at the University of Pittsburgh. He led the Panthers to three consecutive 11–1 seasons and three bowl victories in his first three years. OPPOSITE PAGE: In 1984, Marino became the first quarterback ever to pass for more than 5,000 yards (5,084) in a single season.

DON MAYNARD

WHILE HE NEVER LED THE AFL IN *receiving, Maynard is one of only five players to record 50 or more receptions and more than 1,000 receiving yards five times.*

ecord-setting receiver Don Maynard took an odd road to stardom. It all began with four productive years at tiny Texas Western College, where he was a two-time All-Border Conference halfback and a track star. Maynard was signed by the New York Giants in 1958 but was released after just one season. He then joined the Canadian Football League's Hamilton Tiger-Cats for the 1959 season.

When the American Football League was organized in 1960, Maynard (born 1935) returned to New York with the Titans, a team that would later change its name to the Jets. Don was the first player to sign with the Titans and couldn't have been more pleased with the philosophy of coach Sammy Baugh, who loved to throw the ball. Maynard responded with 72 receptions for 1,265 yards. The Titans and later the Jets struggled for several seasons before they attained any level of respect. Maynard, never a precise pattern runner, often had to "improvise" as one of his team's constantly rotating corp of quarterbacks scrambled for his life.

Not until 1965, when quarterback Joe Namath arrived on the scene, was Don able to develop any sense of quarterback-to-receiver chemistry. That chemistry proved to be the perfect mix in the 1968 AFL title game against the heavily favored Oakland Raiders. The Namath-Maynard combo picked apart the tough Raider defense seemingly at will. Maynard, even though nursing an injury, caught six passes for 118 yards and two touchdowns. "That's the one I'll never forget," Maynard said. "If we hadn't won that day, there would have been no Super Bowl III for us."

While he never led the AFL in receiving, Maynard is one of only five players to record 50 receptions and more than 1,000 receiving yards five times. During his 15-year career with the Giants (1958), Jets (1960–72), and St. Louis Cardinals (1973), he had 100 or more yards receiving in 50 games. His 633 career catches for 11,834 yards were both pro records. Named to the all-time AFL team in 1969, Maynard was accorded the game's highest honor in 1987 when he was elected to the Pro Football Hall of Fame.

MAYNARD WAS RELEASED BY THE NFL'S
*New York Giants in 1958, but be got a
second chance in New York with the
AFL's New York Titans in 1960. The
team was renamed the Jets in '63.*

HUGH McELHENNY

ugh McElhenny was to pro football in the 1950s and early 1960s what Elvis Presley was to rock and roll. Known as "The King" (McElhenny that is), he had it all. He was an artist whose electrifying moves left opponents and observers spellbound.

Born in Los Angeles in 1928, McElhenny began his football career by rewriting the Pacific Coast Conference's record book. The University of Washington All-America halfback established conference records for yards gained (2,499) and longest punt return (100 yards) and led the conference in scoring in 1950 and 1951.

A first-round draft choice of the San Francisco 49ers, McElhenny was an instant hit. His rookie season left sportswriters groping for new superlatives. The versatile back recorded the season's longest run from scrimmage (89 yards), the longest punt return (94 yards), and the top rushing average (7.0 yards per carry). Not surprisingly, he was a unanimous choice for the league's Rookie of the Year honors.

Considered the greatest "thrill runner" of his day, McElhenny ran with a tremendously long stride and high knee action. His breakaway speed and unique ability to change direction at will left defenders dazed and confused.

ABOVE: AFTER NINE SEASONS WITH SAN *Francisco, McElhenny was let go to the expansion Minnesota Vikings in 1961. "The King" responded with 1,067 combined yards and his sixth trip to the Pro Bowl.* **OPPOSITE PAGE:** *A master at open-field running, McElhenny's ability to change direction at will befuddled opponents. He accumulated 11,369 combined rushing, receiving, kickoff return, and punt return yards during his career.*

In 1961, after nine seasons and five Pro Bowl appearances, McElhenny was pawned off to the expansion Minnesota Vikings. It was, all things considered, his finest season. With the Vikings, he accounted for 1,067 combined yards and made his sixth trip to the Pro Bowl.

Two years later, as a member of the New York Giants, McElhenny realized a dream that had thus far escaped him—playing on a championship team. Although Hugh's knees were already shot, Giants coach Allie Sherman knew he would give the team "his very best," something he did automatically his entire 13-year career. When he retired after the 1964 season, McElhenny was one of only three players to have gained more than 11,000 all-purpose yards.

JOE MONTANA

he San Francisco 49ers trailed the Dallas Cowboys 27–21 late in the fourth quarter of the 1981 NFC championship game. Any hope of a 49ers win rested squarely on the shoulders of quarterback Joe Montana. Methodically, he directed the 49er offense 83 yards from their own 11-yard line to the Dallas 6. With just 51 seconds remaining and under a fierce pass rush, the young quarterback fled the safety of the pocket and tossed a high, floating pass toward the back of the end zone. Buried immediately under a mass of Cowboy defenders, Montana didn't see wide receiver Dwight Clark's game-winning grab, known today simply as "The Catch," but the roar of the crowd told him all he needed to know. The 49ers were going to the Super Bowl. It was typical "Montana Magic."

Joe Montana (born 1956) played football, baseball, and basketball for Ringold High School in Monongahela, Pennsylvania, before entering the University of Notre Dame on a football scholarship. Although his statistics at Notre Dame weren't overwhelming, the gutsy play of the "Comeback Kid" was legendary. Still, some questioned his arm strength, and as a result he was not selected by the 49ers until the third round of the 1979 NFL draft.

What scouts overlooked, however, was Montana's natural leadership skills and his almost eerie ability to rally his team from behind. In fact, during his pro career—14 seasons with the 49ers and two with the Kansas City Chiefs—he engineered 31 fourth-quarter comebacks.

With Montana, the 49ers made 10 playoff appearances, captured eight divisional crowns, and won four Super Bowl titles. Their 55–10 thumping of the Denver Broncos in Super Bowl XXIV earned the Niners the right to be called the "Team of the '80s." Leading the assault, as he did in each of the 49ers' three previous Super Bowl victories, was Montana, who completed 22 of 29 passes for 297 yards and five touchdowns. To no one's surprise, he was named Super Bowl MVP for a record third time. A sure-shot Hall of Famer, Montana was named in 1994 to the NFL's 75th Anniversary All-Time Team.

WITH MONTANA AT THE HELM, THE *49ers captured eight divisional crowns and four Super Bowl victories. His Super Bowl numbers: 83 of 122 (68.0 percent), 1,142 yards, 11 TDs, zero interceptions.*

BILL WALSH: "WHEN THE GAME IS ON *the line, and you need someone to go in there and win it right now, I would rather have Joe Montana as my quarterback than anyone who ever played the game."*

MARION MOTLEY

Canton (Ohio) McKinley High School, played in the first-ever high school football game at Fawcett Stadium, home of pro football's annual Hall of Fame Game. OPPOSITE PAGE: The Rams' Tank Younger found out first-hand in the 1950 NFL title game that the Browns and their powerful fullback Motley were no pushovers. Winners of four consecutive AAFC titles (1946–49), the Browns defeated the Rams 30–28.

In 1946, one year before Jackie Robinson signed with baseball's Brooklyn Dodgers, pro football's race barrier was challenged by four players. The trailblazers were Marion Motley and Bill Willis, who signed with the Cleveland Browns of the newly formed All-America Football Conference, and Kenny Washington and Woody Strode, who signed with the NFL's Los Angeles Rams. Injury ended Washington's career after two seasons, while Strode played just the 1946 season. Motley and Willis, however, went on to have Hall of Fame careers.

Motley (born 1920) joined the Browns as a 26-year-old rookie. Coach Paul Brown was already familiar with Motley, having coached the big fullback at the Great Lakes Naval Training Station during World War II. He also knew Motley from his playing days as a high school star in Canton, Ohio. Brown coached football at neighboring Massillon High School.

Marion realized that not everyone in the all-white pro ranks would accept a black player. "Paul addressed that at the first meeting," Motley explained. "He said, 'If you can't get along with your teammates, you won't be here.'" While Motley insists Browns players were supportive, it wasn't always that way around the league. He learned, however, to channel his anger into his play.

At 6'1" and 240 pounds, Marion was an imposing figure. While he was quick and agile, he preferred to attack defenders straight on. When quarterback Otto Graham had trouble finding an open receiver, he sought out Motley. Together, they established the fullback as an effective receiver. The draw play, now a staple in every NFL team's offensive arsenal, began with Motley and Graham.

Motley, the AAFC's all-time leading rusher, led the NFL in rushing in 1950. That year, in a game against Pittsburgh, he gained 188 yards on just 11 carries for a 17.1 yards-per-carry average. In his nine professional seasons, he amassed 4,720 yards on 828 carries for an amazing 5.7 yards per carry. A 1968 Hall of Fame inductee, Motley was named to the NFL's All-Time Team in 1994.

ANTHONY MUNOZ

ABOVE: MUNOZ MAINTAINED A STRICT *year-round conditioning program that included working out in the weight room he had installed in his home.* **OPPOSITE PAGE:** *Although no one would ever confuse Munoz with any of the speedy receivers of the day, he did score four touchdowns during his career on tackle-eligible plays.*

F ew historians would argue that Anthony Munoz was the best offensive tackle to play the game in recent history. Some, like former Cincinnati Bengals head coach Sam Wyche, go even further. "Anthony is a better person than he was a player," Wyche said. "And he was one of the greatest players of all time. That is what heroes are suppose to look like and act like."

Munoz (born 1958) did everything an offensive lineman should do in superior ways. An exceptional straight-on blocker, he was agile, quick, and strong. In 1987, he played in 11 games and allowed just one and one-half sacks. His stalwart play was the key to the success that propelled Cincinnati to two Super Bowls during his 13-year career. "There are no comparisons between him and other tackles," remarked All-Pro defensive end Bruce Smith. "He has proven year after year that he is the best."

Munoz, who earned All-America honors in 1978 and '79 at the University of Southern California, was the Bengals' first-round pick in the 1980 NFL draft. Some considered the pick a risk because of a knee injury Munoz had sustained in college. But as the celebrated Bengals lineman proved, the concerns were unfounded. Munoz started 177 of 178 games from 1980–91. Even when his team did poorly, Munoz played with consistent excellence. He set high personal standards and worked tirelessly to achieve them. A terrific all-around athlete, he even scored four touchdowns during his career on tackle-eligible pass plays.

The recipient of virtually every possible honor, Anthony played in 11 consecutive Pro Bowls and was named NFL Offensive Lineman of the Year by one organization or another in 1981, 1982, and 1985–89. In 1994, he was selected to the NFL's 75th Anniversary All-Time Team. But perhaps the most fitting of his many honors was being named the recipient of the NFL Man of the Year Award in 1991. Given to players who excel as role models both on and off the field, the honor couldn't have been bestowed upon a more appropriate person.

BRONKO NAGURSKI

One day, Bronko Nagurski took a handoff, blasted through the opposition, crossed the goal line, and ran clear through the end zone and into a brick wall. "That last guy hit me awfully hard," he admitted later.

A charter member of the Pro Football Hall of Fame, Nagurski (1908–1990) symbolized power running to fans during the 1930s, and many eyewitnesses still insist that for sheer brutal line-smashing, the great Chicago Bears fullback has never been matched. Never fancy, he didn't dance, jiggle, or juke; he just plowed straight ahead—right through people. His style was the stuff of legends. When one coach was asked how he planned to stop Nagurski, he shrugged: "With a shotgun as he's leaving the locker room."

IN THE EARLY 1930S, THE CHICAGO *Bears featured the ultimate dream backfield: Red Grange (left) and Nagurski (right). A two-yard Nagurski to Grange touchdown pass helped Chicago beat Portsmouth for the 1932 NFL championship, 9–0.*

More than a great runner, Bronko was a complete player. At the University of Minnesota, he played four positions and was named an All-American at both fullback and tackle. With the Bears, his linebacking was as fearsome as his line-bucking. His blocking might have made him All-Pro had he never even carried the ball.

His jump-pass off a fake line plunge was devastating. It went for the key touchdown in the Bears' 1932 victory over Portsmouth for the league championship. The next year, in the NFL's first official championship game, Bronko passed for two touchdowns, including the one that scored the game-winning points.

When he couldn't get a raise to $6,500 in 1938, Nagurski retired to become a professional wrestler. But in 1943, when war demands left the Bears short on manpower, he rejoined the team as a tackle. Late in the season, with Chicago trailing in a must-win game, he went back to fullback. Again and again, the 35-year-old Bronko tore into the line. His mighty plunges keyed a drive to the tying touchdown and then set up the winning score. A week later, he scored a touchdown to help the Bears win the championship game. Then he retired for good.

NAGURSKI, AN ALL-AMERICAN AT *both fullback and tackle at the University of Minnesota, was used primarily as a fullback on offense by the Bears. However, six seasons after he retired, Nagurski returned to pro football for one final season as a tackle.*

JOE NAMATH

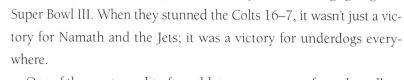

The Miami Touchdown Club had just presented New York Jets quarterback Joe Namath its award as professional football's Player of the Year. Suddenly, a fan yelled that the Baltimore Colts were, in so many words, going to beat the Jets in the upcoming Super Bowl. Namath responded by saying, "We're going to win Sunday. I guarantee you."

Most of the media dismissed the remark as just another case of Broadway Joe's notorious bravado. It wasn't. "A lot of us felt we weren't getting respect," he said. "We were tired of hearing that stuff." The Jets were 19½-point underdogs going into Super Bowl III. When they stunned the Colts 16–7, it wasn't just a victory for Namath and the Jets; it was a victory for underdogs everywhere.

One of the most sought-after athletes ever to come from the college ranks, Namath led the University of Alabama to three banner seasons during which they lost only three regular-season games. Alabama coach Bear Bryant called his star quarterback "the greatest athlete I ever coached." Joe was drafted in the first round by teams in both the American Football League and NFL. His decision to sign with the AFL's Jets was the turning point in the costly war between the rival leagues. Eighteen months later, a merger was in place.

ABOVE: NAMATH THREW FOR TWO *touchdowns in this December 16, 1973, matchup against the Bills, but it was O. J. Simpson who stole the show. Simpson rushed for 200 yards and became the first player to gain 2,000 yards in a season.* **OPPOSITE PAGE:** *Namath's most productive game came on September 24, 1972, when he riddled the Colts for 496 passing yards and six touchdowns.*

In the pros, Namath (born 1943) repeatedly demonstrated his tremendous abilities. In an injury-plagued 13-season career with the Jets (1965–76) and Los Angeles Rams (1977), the masterful passer threw for 27,663 yards and 173 touchdowns. The slope-shouldered quarterback amassed 300- and 400-yard games when such accomplishments weren't so commonplace. He registered six 300-yard games in 1967, four in 1968, and three more in 1969. He passed for more than 3,000 yards in three of his first four seasons, and in 1967 he became the first to pass for more than 4,000 yards in a season. Selected to play in five AFL All-Star Games or AFC/NFC Pro Bowls, he was inducted into the Pro Football Hall of Fame in 1985.

ERNIE NEVERS

f all the records in NFL history, the one that has survived the longest was set on November 28, 1929, when the Chicago Cardinals' big, blond fullback, Ernie Nevers, slammed across six touchdowns and kicked four PATs for every one of his team's points in a 40–6 rout of the arch-rival Bears. Yet that performance was only one of many herculean achievements in Nevers's remarkable career.

At Stanford University, his coach, Pop Warner, called him "the football player without a fault" and compared him favorably with an earlier Warner protégé—Jim Thorpe! Like Thorpe, Nevers (1903–1976) could do everything on a football field exceptionally well—run, pass, kick, call signals, and play rock-hard defense. Equally important, he topped it all with a blazing competitive spirit. Only two broken ankles kept him from All-America recognition in 1924, yet he came back limping late in the season to star against Notre Dame's "Four Horsemen" in the Rose Bowl. Healthy the next year, he made everyone's honor team.

In 1926, Red Grange formed his own pro football league as a rival to the NFL. When Nevers turned pro with the Eskimos of Duluth, Minnesota, he immediately became the NFL's biggest drawing card. The Eskimos were a touring team, spotlighting big Ernie's skills in every league city as a counter to Grange's appeal. So no one would miss the point, the team was renamed "Ernie Nevers's Eskimos."

It was quite a season. The Eskimos crossed the country, playing 29 games against league and nonleague opponents. Nevers played an incredible 1,713 minutes of football. The big crowds the Eskimos drew helped the NFL win the "war" against Grange's league. The 1927 season saw another tour. In two years, Nevers played as much football as many played in a half-dozen.

Nevers took a season off to assist coach Warner at Stanford, then joined the Chicago Cardinals for three more years. In his five NFL seasons, the only important All-Pro team he missed was one chosen by the modest star himself for a Midwest newspaper.

IN 1926, NEVERS'S DULUTH ESKIMOS
played 29 games, 28 of them on the road. Nevers played all but 27 of a possible 1,713 minutes.

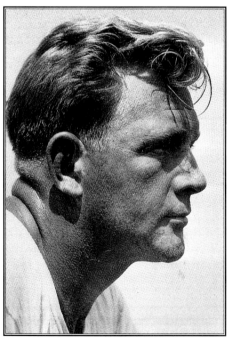

IN ADDITION TO SCORING A RECORD *40 points against the Bears on November 28, 1929, Nevers scored all of his team's points again the next week for a two-week total of 59 solo points.*

RAY NITSCHKE

ay Nitschke, according to Hall of Fame quarterback and teammate Bart Starr, was "a classic example of Dr. Jekyll and Mr. Hyde." Off the field, he was a thoughtful, caring person. On the field, he was a ferocious middle linebacker who at times seemed to truly enjoy hitting people. A fierce competitor, Ray was the heart of the great Green Bay Packers defense of the 1960s.

Born in 1936, Ray had to overcome a great deal of personal adversity at an early age. His father was killed when he was three and his mother died when he was 13. He was adopted and raised by an older brother. It was his brother who convinced him to turn down a $3,000 baseball contract from the St. Louis Browns in favor of attending the University of Illinois. "It was the smartest thing I ever did," Ray said.

At Illinois, Nitschke played fullback on offense and linebacker on defense. The Packers drafted him in 1958 as a linebacker. Although he started eight games as a rookie, it wasn't until his third season that Nitschke got the job of middle linebacker for good. Under fiery head coach Vince Lombardi, he quickly developed into a player who epitomized the hard-nosed style of those great Packers teams that played in six championship games and won the first two Super Bowls. "The guy never let up," Nitschke recalled of Lombardi. "But he was consistent. . . . He wanted me to not only be a good player but to be a good guy. I needed that."

Nitschke was a complete player. In addition to being a hard-hitting tackler, he was excellent in pass coverage as his 25 lifetime interceptions attest. In the 1962 title game, Ray recovered two fumbles and deflected a pass as the Packers defeated the New York Giants 16–7 in minus-20-degree windchill conditions. For his efforts, he was named the game's MVP. In 1978, Nitschke became the first Green Bay defender from the 1960s to be elected to the Hall of Fame.

NITSCHKE AND VINCE LOMBARDI

watch the Packers' offense perform during the 1967 NFL Western Conference playoff game. The Nitschke-led defense smothered the Rams in the second half as the Packers pounded out a 28–7 win.

ONE OF THE HARDEST HITTING *linebackers ever, Nitschke was also quick enough to intercept 25 passes during his career.*

LEO NOMELLINI

The only problem San Francisco 49ers coaches had with Leo Nomellini in 14 seasons was deciding whether he was more valuable on offense or defense. As a blocker, the 6'3", 264-pound giant opened huge holes in defensive lines and had the agility to drop back and defend 49ers passers as well as any tackle in the league. On defense, he was an avalanche of a pass rusher and equally adept at stuffing enemy runners.

All-Pro selectors had a similar problem. He was chosen for offensive honors in 1951 and 1952 and on defense in 1953, '54, '57, and '59. He was picked for 10 Pro Bowls in his first 12 seasons, starting at times on either side of the line. Through most of his career, he showed up on either platoon in an important situation. In 1955, when injuries decimated both San Francisco lines, "The Lion" played virtually 60 minutes a game all season.

Injuries never stopped Nomellini. Born in Lucca, Italy, in 1924, he was a consensus All-American at the University of Minnesota in 1949. The 49ers made him their first draft choice in 1950, and he never missed a game until he retired after the 1963 season—174 straight games.

The 49ers had numerous stars in addition to Leo during Nomellini's tenure. Their entire starting backfield of 1954—Y. A. Tittle, Hugh McElhenny, John Henry Johnson, and Joe Perry—has been enshrined in the Pro Football Hall of Fame. Yet they never seemed to have a complete team. One year, the offense would be spectacular but the defense would be poor. When the defense was strong, the offense would go flat. It made the decision of where to play Nomellini all the more important—and all the more impossible.

During off-seasons, Nomellini wrestled professionally around the Bay area. He learned to use some of his "wrasslin' show" on the football field. Before the ball was snapped, he'd assault opponents with huffs, puffs, growls, snorts, and other animal sounds, all the while screwing his face into a horrible mask. Of course, if that didn't scare the opponent to death, Leo would just flatten him.

AN ALL-AMERICA TACKLE AT MINNE-
sota, Nomellini also participated in track, putting the shot and—as unlikely as it may seem—running the anchor leg on the 440-yard relay team.

NOMELLINI WAS NAMED ALL-PRO ON *both offense and defense. He won offensive recognition in 1951 and 1952 and defensive honors in 1953, '54, '57, and '59.*

MERLIN OLSEN

Merlin Olsen was everything a coach could want in a defensive tackle. He was big, strong, agile, and a natural leader. His physical tools earned him the Outland Trophy and All-America honors as a collegian at Utah State. As a pro with the Los Angeles Rams (1962–76), the 6′5″, 270-pound lineman was named to the Pro Bowl an unprecedented 14 times.

A Phi Beta Kappa at Utah State, Olsen (born 1940) placed a high value on education. During the off-season while playing for the Rams, he earned a master's degree in economics. A clean player, he never subscribed to the philosophy that you had to "hate" your opponent to reach the necessary emotional level to defeat him. "If you are motivated by pride and the desire to win," he stated, "you will want to dominate your opponent, but that is a lot better than hatred on which to tie your success."

For 10 years, Olsen's partner on the left side of the line was the flamboyant Deacon Jones. Together, the two future Hall of Famers were unstoppable. They were joined by Lamar Lundy, Rosey Grier, and later Roger Brown to form a unit known as the "Fearsome Foursome." In the 1960s, with Olsen as their leader, the Fearsome Foursome were the terror of the NFL. "We never had a bad game from Merlin," Rams coach George Allen once remarked. "We always got a good game and, more often than not, a great game."

Throughout his career, Olsen skillfully merged his physical tools with his authoritative style. By the late 1960s, retirements and trades began to break up the Fearsome Foursome. New additions to the line looked to Olsen to be the "glue" that would hold them together. It was a job he accepted willingly and performed effectively. "Jones was the inspirational force of the Foursome," suggested Rams defensive line coach Sid Hall, "but Oley provided the leadership."

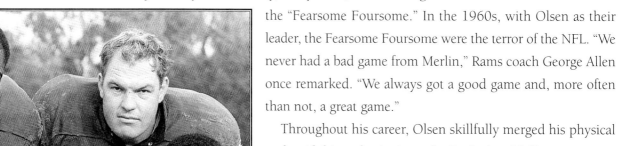

BELOW: THE RAMS' "FEARSOME *Foursome" of (clockwise) Lamar Lundy, Olsen, Deacon Jones, and Roger Brown. Olsen was the stabilizer in the middle who allowed the others free reign to tee off on passers.* **OPPOSITE PAGE:** *Olsen was selected to a record 14 Pro Bowls during his 15 NFL seasons. Extremely durable, the big tackle played 208 games for the Rams—the last 198 consecutively.*

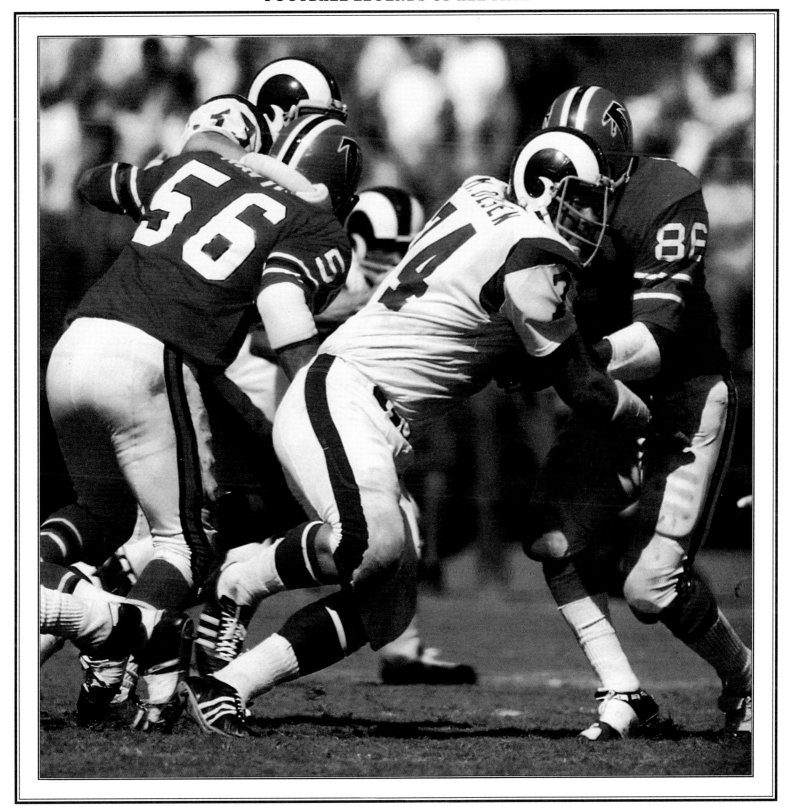

ALAN PAGE

career, Page became a judge on the Minnesota Supreme Court. Here he finds Cardinal Terry Metcalf guilty of fumbling. **OPPOSITE PAGE:** *Bears quarterback Bobby Douglass barely has time to turn before Page is in his face. In an unusual switch, Page became lighter as his career progressed, trading weight for speed and quickness.*

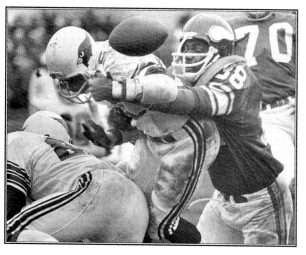

Minnesota Supreme Court Justice Alan Page is known for his aggressive, no-nonsense style. That style served the University of Minnesota Law School graduate well during his "other" career as a defensive tackle for the Minnesota Vikings and Chicago Bears.

"If you're going to make a mistake," Page once said, "make it aggressively." That assertive approach made him one of the most effective defensive players of his era. It also contributed to some pretty impressive career statistics, including 23 opponent fumble recoveries, 28 blocked kicks, and 173 quarterback sacks.

Page, who was born in 1945 in Canton, Ohio, home of the Pro Football Hall of Fame, won a scholarship to Notre Dame. There he earned All-America honors as a senior. The Fighting Irish standout was the Vikings' No. 1 pick in the 1967 NFL draft. He earned the starting right defensive tackle job in his fourth game and remained a regular throughout the rest of his 238-game career. In 1972, he became the first defensive player selected the NFL's Most Valuable Player, and he was the NFC Defensive Player of the Year four other times. The nine-time Pro Bowl performer was a major contributor to Viking squads that won 10 NFL/NFC Central Division championships.

Page combined speed and agility to knife past the opposition. Rather than wait for the ball carrier, he sought him out. "A defensive player should think of himself more as an aggressor, not as a defender," he explained.

The 6'4", 278-pound Page gradually pared down his weight to 225 through a rigorous running routine. Vikings coach Bud Grant, however, believed Page's weight loss hurt his performance. Grant placed him on waivers after the sixth game of the 1978 season. The Bears contacted him within hours of his release. Although he joined Chicago in midseason, he led all Bear defenders with 11½ sacks. He played three more seasons with the Bears before calling it quits in 1981. In 1988, the Canton native returned home for induction into the Hall of Fame.

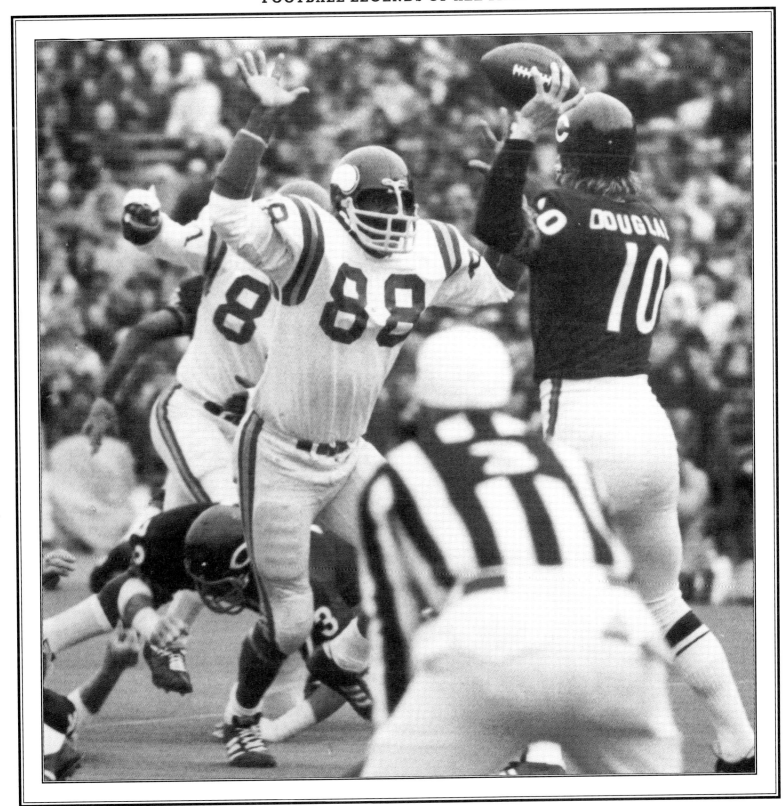

JIM PARKER

im Parker was called "Johnny Unitas's bodyguard." As soon as he joined the Baltimore Colts in 1957, he learned the "one big rule"—protect the team's great passer. Coach Weeb Ewbank told him bluntly: "You can be the most unpopular man on the team if the quarterback gets hurt."

Parker (born 1934) always maintained his popularity with his teammates, although quite a few defensive linemen around the NFL were less than fond of him. At Ohio State, the 6'3", 275-pound Parker was a two-way player and winner of the 1956 Outland Trophy as the nation's outstanding lineman. When the Colts drafted him No. 1 in 1957, most observers expected Baltimore to plug him into its defensive line. At OSU, famous for its "three yards and a cloud of dust" running attack, he had little chance to pass block, a skill essential for a pro offensive lineman.

WHEN A 1967 KNEE INJURY FAILED TO *respond, Parker might have hung on through the season collecting paychecks. Instead, he retired so as not to hurt the team by taking up a roster spot.*

However, coach Ewbank placed him at offensive left tackle, the key position in protecting Unitas from "blind side" blitzers. In Parker's first game, the Colts threw 47 passes—"more that day than we did all my four years at Ohio State," Parker remembered. Big Jim quickly mastered the intricacies of pass blocking. By the end of his rookie year, *The Sporting News* named him to its All-Western Conference team.

After several years as an All-Pro tackle, Parker was switched to left guard, a completely different position requiring him to pull and lead-block on outside running plays. Although the defensive tackles he took on were bigger than the defensive ends he had faced as an offensive tackle, Parker always maintained he preferred blocking the bigger but slower tackles.

Parker put together an unusual eight-year streak as an All-Pro performer—four years as a tackle and four more as a guard. He was also chosen to eight Pro Bowls. Six years after his 1967 retirement, he was inducted into the Pro Football Hall of Fame as the first "pure" offensive lineman to be so honored.

PARKER STARRED AS A SOPHOMORE
with Ohio State's national championship team of 1954. Here, Buckeyes Parker, Hubert Bobo, and Jack Archer (left to right) leave the muddy field after their 20–7 Rose Bowl win over USC.

WALTER PAYTON

Walter Payton, the NFL's all-time leading rusher, was arguably the best running back to play the game. "When Walter went down the assembly line," a Chicago Bears assistant coach once remarked, "everything was a chrome-plated part."

A remarkable athlete, Payton (born 1954) didn't play organized football until his junior year at Columbia (Mississippi) High School. But he ran 65 yards for a touchdown on his first carry and scored on a 75-yard play later the same game. Recruited by several major colleges, he chose Jackson State so that he could play in the same backfield as his brother Eddie. At Jackson State, Walter rushed for 3,563 yards in four seasons and scored 464 points. It was there that he earned the nickname "Sweetness," because of his smooth running style.

For 13 seasons with the Bears, Payton mesmerized observers with his spectacular play. He had the speed to run outside plus the power to drive up the middle. Exceptionally durable, he missed only one game in his rookie season and then played in 186 consecutive games. His astonishing durability helped him establish NFL records for carries (3,838), yards gained (16,726), and rushing touchdowns (110). A complete football player, he was a devastating blocker and caught 492 passes for 4,538 yards and 15 touchdowns. His best single-game performance occurred on November 20, 1977, when he rushed for 275 yards against the Minnesota Vikings. That same season, he ran for a career-best 1,852 yards.

A punishing runner, Payton rarely ran out of bounds. He explained: "My coach at Jackson State, Bob Hill, always said that if you are going to die, you should die hard, never die easy." Despite all the attention and honors bestowed upon him during his extraordinary career, Payton always maintained a healthy perspective. Upon learning of his election to the Hall of Fame, he humbly remarked, "I'm thrilled but embarrassed. I got paid for playing a kid's game, and I enjoyed it."

BELOW: ALTHOUGH HE RECEIVED *little national publicity at Jackson State, Payton became the leading scorer in NCAA history with 464 points while rushing for 3,563 yards.* **OPPOSITE PAGE:** *Payton owns nearly all of the NFL career rushing records. His teammates respected him for his leadership and all-around play. His superior blocking added yards to teammates' totals, and he was also a dangerous option passer.*

JERRY RICE

ABOVE: THE MOMENT OF TRUTH:
Rice's total concentration is on the football, yet at the same moment he prepares to escape a defender's tackle. That incredible ability has enabled him to shatter touchdown records. **OPPOSITE PAGE:** *Like a good wine, Rice improves with age. Here he performs his magic against the baffled Cowboys in a 1996 game. At age 34, he led the NFL with 108 catches.*

The San Francisco 49ers were heavy favorites to defeat the Cincinnati Bengals in Super Bowl XXIII. But as the fourth quarter began, they were trailing 13–6. It began to look as though the Bengals were about to pull off a huge upset. But then 49ers wide receiver Jerry Rice took over.

On the fourth play of the 49ers' first drive of the final quarter, Rice leaped high into the air to snag a Joe Montana pass. As he came down, he stretched his 6'2" frame forward just enough to cross the Cincinnati goal line for the tying score. But the determined Bengals answered with a field goal to take the lead 16–13. Rice went back to work. This time, with just 1:15 remaining, he turned a short Montana toss into a 27-yard gain to the Cincinnati 18-yard line. Two plays later, he streaked across the middle of the field. The Bengals secondary, fearing his speed and athletic ability, adjusted and double-teamed him. This left John Taylor wide open for the touchdown throw. Respect for Jerry Rice had thus set up the game-winning touchdown pass. His 11 catches for a Super Bowl-record 215 yards earned him MVP honors.

Rice (born 1962) was the 49ers' No. 1 draft choice in 1985. He had attended tiny Mississippi Valley State, where he established 18 NCAA Division II records. Named to the NFL's 75th Anniversary All-Time Team, he holds virtually every meaningful NFL receiving mark.

Many experts contend that Rice is the greatest receiver the game has produced. His impressive credentials include 11 Pro Bowl selections, 11 consecutive 1,000-yard receiving seasons, and three 100-catch seasons. A virtual scoring machine, he caught an NFL-record 22 touchdown passes in the strike-shortened 1987 season and a career-record 154 in just 11 seasons. It took the previous record-holder, Hall of Famer Steve Largent, 14 seasons to collect 100 touchdown passes. It's no wonder former 49ers head coach Bill Walsh called Jerry Rice "the most dominating player in the game today."

EDDIE ROBINSON

O n October 5, 1985, at the Cotton Bowl in Dallas, Grambling State University defeated Prairie View A&M 27–7. The victory made Grambling's Eddie Robinson college football's all-time winningest coach, as he surpassed Bear Bryant's 323 wins.

Two years earlier, unable to make an airplane connection, Robinson (born 1919) had driven 400 miles to attend Bryant's funeral. Questioned about the record, Robinson said, "I don't want to be remembered as the guy who broke Bryant's record any more than Bryant wanted to be remembered as the man who broke (Amos Alonzo) Stagg's record. I would like to be remembered as a guy who made the same contributions Bryant did, who influenced people's lives and made an impact on the game."

For all his victories—he surpassed 400 in 1995—it will undoubtedly be Robinson's ability to exert a positive influence on his players that will last long after the numbers are taken down from the scoreboard. A superb teacher of football, Robinson is an even greater teacher of life.

"When I left Grambling," Doug Williams, Washington's winning quarterback in Super Bowl XXII, said, "I felt like I had a degree in philosophy. It is amazing what that man knows, in addition to all the football he teaches."

A TENSE MOMENT FOR ROBINSON IN *a 1973 playoff game against Western Kentucky. The game saw Grambling take a rare loss, 28–20.*

Hall of Famer Willie Davis remembered: "Whether Eddie was coming through the dormitory checking on your work habits or getting athletes out to class, this thing was extremely important to him. He was always someone you could go to to discuss a personal problem and come away with the feeling you'd been with someone who showed sensitivity and understanding."

Robinson first came to Grambling in 1941 as head football (and basketball) coach for a salary of $63.75 a month. Over the years, he's sent many players on to the NFL, including four members of the Pro Football Hall of Fame. Virtually to a man, they and those whose football ended with their final college game agree they were better for having played for Robinson.

ROBINSON WAS A HANDS-ON COACH *who always cared about his players' whole college experience, not just the time spent on the football field. By the end of 1996, Robinson had sent 98 players to the NFL.*

KNUTE ROCKNE

More than 60 years after his death in an airplane crash in a Kansas wheat field, Knute Rockne of Notre Dame is still the most famous football coach in history. Perhaps no coach, not even "Rock" himself, could live up to the legend he left behind.

His locker room orations were famous. A master psychologist, he believed that the right word to a player was sometimes more important than hours of practice time. His "win one for the Gipper" speech in 1928 brought an underdog Notre Dame squad victory over powerful Army. On another occasion, when the Irish trailed at halftime, his players sat in the locker room dreading their coach's appearance. At the last second, the door flew open and Rockne yelled, "Let's go, girls!" The team stormed onto the field and triumphed.

But Rockne's success was based on more than words. His practices were meticulous. Plays were run over and over until the timing was perfect. His philosophy emphasized speed, timing, deception, and quick-opening plays over brawn. Many of his greatest players, including the "Four Horsemen" backfield that took the Irish to the Rose Bowl in 1925, were much smaller than their opponents. He employed outstanding assistants such as the famous line coach Hunk Anderson. Many of his assistants as well as many of his players went on to coaching success in college and pro football.

Born in Norway, Rockne (1888–1931) was an undersized end at Notre Dame in 1913 when he starred in one of the most important games ever. The forward pass had been legalized in 1906, but few important teams took it seriously until Rockne and quarterback Gus Dorais used it to lead then little-known Notre Dame over Army in an astounding upset. From that point on, the pass grew in importance as an offensive weapon.

As Notre Dame coach from 1918–30, Rockne compiled a magnificent 105–12–5 record, including a 1925 Rose Bowl win over Stanford. Three of his teams—1924, 1929, and 1930—were ranked as national champions.

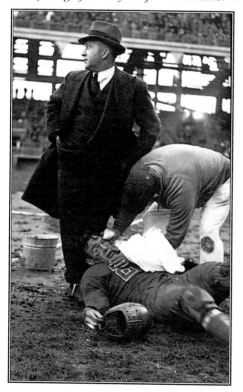

ROCKNE CHECKS ON AN INJURED
player during a game. Genuinely concerned about his players, he helped many long after they'd left Notre Dame.

AT THE HEIGHT OF THE DEPRESSION, *Rockne called together an All-Star team of his former players to play the New York Giants for charity. The Giants won, but the game raised $115,000.*

BARRY SANDERS

BELOW: BECAUSE HE'S RELATIVELY *small for an NFL running back, Sanders is often replaced by a bigger back when the Lions get inside an opponent's 10-yard line. But, with few in-close touchdowns, he ran for 84 six-pointers through 1996.* **OPPOSITE PAGE:** *Sanders eludes a Packers defender in a 1996 game—his eighth straight season of over 1,000 yards rushing. His 1,553 yards gave him his third NFL rushing title.*

N o one in the NFL today forces game-plan adjustments like the Detroit Lions' Barry Sanders. Since joining the Lions in 1989, following a three-year career at Oklahoma State, his accomplishments have been nothing short of spectacular.

Sanders (born 1968) began as an understudy to All-America halfback Thurman Thomas at OSU. When Thomas departed for the NFL, Sanders, a junior, assumed the starter's role. That season, the soft-spoken Wichita, Kansas, native electrified the nation as he demolished seven major NCAA single-season records, including rushing yards (2,628) and touchdowns (37). Of course, he won the Heisman Trophy.

After foregoing his senior season, Sanders made his pro debut just three days after signing with the Lions, who had made him their first-round pick. He absolutely dazzled a Pontiac Silverdome crowd when he darted and dashed for an 18-yard gain on his first NFL carry. But that was just the beginning. His 1,470 yards rushing that season was a Lions record and just 10 yards short of the league's best for the year. The following season, the sophomore pro seized the rushing crown with 1,304 yards, and he demonstrated his versatility by racking up another 462 yards receiving.

His best season, however, was 1994, when he rushed for 1,883 yards. It was the fourth-highest single-season rushing total in NFL history.

Though not big by most standards, the speedy, 5'8" Sanders capitalizes on his size by running low to the ground, making himself less of a target for would-be tacklers. He runs so low, in fact, that at times he seems to defy gravity.

A brilliant performer, Barry Sanders is considered by many to be the premier running back in the NFL today. In 1996, he became just the eighth player in NFL history to rush for over 11,000 yards. He is one of only two running backs to have gained more than 1,000 yards in each of his first eight seasons, joining his old friend and college teammate, Thomas, in that exclusive club.

GALE SAYERS

opened a few eyes and set an unbreakable NCAA record when he burst 99 yards from scrimmage for a touchdown against arch rival Nebraska.
OPPOSITE PAGE: *Sayers leaps over a fallen teammate. One year, when the Bears' blocking was particularly weak, a commentator said Sayers might become the "first man to be named All-Pro for turning three-yard losses into one-yard gains."*

"I f you wish to see perfection at running back," remarked Chicago Bears owner George Halas, "you'd best get a hold of a film of Gale Sayers." The occasion for Halas's high praise was Sayers's 1977 Pro Football Hall of Fame induction ceremony.

The youngest man ever accorded pro football's highest honor, Sayers (born 1943) began his remarkable career as a standout halfback at the University of Kansas. The exciting "Kansas Comet" was one of the most brilliant performers in the Big Eight Conference's history. In three seasons, he rushed for 2,675 yards, returned 22 kickoffs for 513 yards, brought back 28 punts for 324 yards, and caught 35 passes for 408 yards. His 283 yards rushing in a 1962 game against Oklahoma State and his 99-yard run from scrimmage against Nebraska in 1963 were both conference records.

As a pro, Sayers exploded on the scene. His trademark moves and breakaway speed dazzled his Chicago Bears teammates, opponents, and fans alike. In a game against the Vikings midway into his remarkable rookie season, Sayers scored four touchdowns, one coming on a 96-yard kickoff return. A few weeks later, the amazing rookie scored an NFL record-tying six touchdowns against the San Francisco 49ers. Sayers's one-man show included an 80-yard pass-run play, a 50-yard rush, and an 85-yard punt return. For the season, he amassed 2,272 combined net yards and scored an NFL rookie-record 22 touchdowns.

In 1966, Sayers increased his net yards figure to an NFL-record 2,440 yards and led the league in rushing with 1,231 yards. After an outstanding campaign in 1967 and a great nine-game start (856 yards rushing) in 1968, Sayers suffered a season-ending knee injury. Determined to resume where he left off, Sayers battled back. In 1969, the Comeback Player of the Year rushed for a league-best 1,032 yards. But injuries continued to take their toll and, just before the start of the 1972 season, Sayers called it quits.

JOE SCHMIDT

ABOVE: IN 1953, THE STEELERS *planned to draft Schmidt on the seventh round. The Lions, drafting just before Pittsburgh, chose a player but a Steelers official hopped up and yelled that the player was ineligible. Detroit then selected Schmidt.* **OPPOSITE PAGE:** *Schmidt sacks the Rams' Roman Gabriel in a 37–17 Lions win in 1964. Best known as a run stopper, Schmidt could blitz quarterbacks with the best of them. He also had 24 career interceptions.*

Contrary to popular opinion, Detroit's Joe Schmidt did not invent the middle linebacker position; he just played it better than it had ever been played before. Few have played the spot better since.

In his first two seasons with the Lions, 1953 and '54, the former University of Pittsburgh star played as an outside linebacker in the then-prevalent 5–2 defense (five linemen, two linebackers). But when a weakness developed up the center, Detroit coach Buddy Parker switched to a 4–3 with Schmidt moving into the middle.

The 4–3 required an unusually versatile middle linebacker. He needed to be strong enough to move into the line and stop running plays, quick and agile enough to evade 250-pound blockers and run down plays to the outside, fast enough to drop back to cover pass receivers, and smart enough to diagnose enemy plays before they developed.

It was a big order, but the 6'0", 222-pound Schmidt (born 1932) filled it admirably. The Lions won the NFL championship in his rookie season and the division title in 1954. Two frustrating seasons followed, but in 1957 the Lions were back in the championship game. Their 59–14 dismantling of the Cleveland Browns was one of the most one-sided routs ever seen in the long history of NFL title tilts. Schmidt and company held the great Jim Brown to only 69 rushing yards.

Schmidt's college career had been checkered. He returned an intercepted pass 60 yards to help upset Notre Dame 22–19, and he received some All-America mention as a senior. But mostly he'd been dogged by injuries. The Lions waited until the seventh round before drafting him because they questioned his durability.

During his 13-year NFL career, Schmidt developed middle linebacker into the dominant pro defensive position, setting the standard for later outstanding middle men like Sam Huff, Ray Nitschke, and Jack Lambert. He was All-NFL nine times and chosen for nine consecutive Pro Bowls. In 1973, he was named to the Pro Football Hall of Fame.

DON SHULA

is carried off the field after defeating the Rams for the NFL's Western Division title in 1964. Despite its gaudy 12–2 record, Baltimore was upset by Cleveland in the championship game. **OPPOSITE PAGE:** *A happy team of Dolphins cheers its coach as he wins his 325th game—the all-time NFL record—a 19–14 edging of the Philadelphia Eagles on November 14, 1993.*

O n November 14, 1993, when the Miami Dolphins defeated the Philadelphia Eagles 19–14, Don Shula became the winningest coach in NFL history. His amazing 325 career victories surpassed the legendary George Halas's record of 324 wins. By the time he retired following the 1995 season, Shula had amassed a seemingly unmatchable 347 career victories.

Shula (born 1930) began his football career as a running back at John Carroll University in Cleveland. He played pro ball with the Cleveland Browns (1951 and 1952), the Baltimore Colts (1953–56), and the Washington Redskins (1957). Used primarily as a defensive back, the Grand River, Ohio, native recorded 21 career interceptions.

A dedicated student of the game, Shula began his 32-year career as a head coach in the NFL in 1963, as the new man in charge of the Baltimore Colts. Under Shula, the Colts rose from fourth place in the NFL's Western Conference to conference champions in just two seasons. In seven seasons, Shula's Colts never finished below second place in their division. In 1970, he left the Colts to take over the leadership reins of the young Miami Dolphins.

Again Shula worked his magic, transforming the 3–10–1 Dolphins into a playoff qualifier his first season and laying the foundation for a perennial contender. His ultimate achievement, however, was the Dolphins' 1972 undefeated season that climaxed with a 14–7 win over the Washington Redskins in Super Bowl VII. Not too surprisingly, Shula lists that game as his No. 1 career highlight. "That win capped our perfect 17–0 season, an accomplishment that had never been achieved before and hasn't been duplicated since," he said.

A master of preparation, a Don Shula team was always dressed and ready to go. In 26 seasons as Miami's head coach, the Dolphins registered just one losing season. During that same stretch, the Dolphins were pro football's winningest team. Elected to the Hall of Fame in 1997, Shula is without a doubt the standard by which all future NFL coaches will be measured.

O. J. SIMPSON

in the 1973 season finale against the Jets to break Jim Brown's single-season rushing mark, but he didn't stop there. His 200-yard game made him the first to run for 2,000 yards in a season. **OPPOSITE PAGE:** *Amazingly, one of Simpson's early pro coaches seriously considered switching one of football's greatest runners to wide receiver. When Lou Saban became Buffalo's coach in 1972, his ground-oriented offense was perfect for Simpson.*

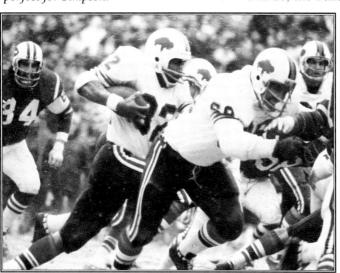

His trial and controversial acquittal for the murders of his ex-wife, Nicole Brown, and Ron Goldman permanently destroyed Simpson's carefully crafted image as one of the good guys. But, though his popularity as "The Juice" is now irretrievable, the record he created in the 1970s as one of pro football's great runners remains unassailable.

Orenthal James Simpson (born 1947) was the 1968 Heisman Trophy winner and a two-time All-American at USC. The 6'1", 200-pound halfback had everything one could ask for in a runner—terrific speed, a mystifying change of pace, surprising power, and more moves than a hula line. The Buffalo Bills made him the No. 1 pick in the 1969 NFL draft. But when he failed to rush for as many as 750 yards in any of his first three seasons with the Bills, he was considered a major disappointment.

The problem was how he was being used—sparingly. In quest of a balanced offense, the Buffalo coaches severely restricted the number of carries Simpson had each game. One Bills coach even wanted to switch him to wide receiver! Then Lou Saban took over as Buffalo coach in 1972 and everything changed. Simpson began running the ball 25–30 times a game. In his first year under Saban, O. J. had his first of five straight 1,000-yard seasons. During that five-year period, Simpson won four NFL rushing titles.

In 1973, Simpson rushed for 2,003 yards to become the first player ever to top the two-grand barrier. He averaged 6.0 yards per carry on 332 attempts and scored 12 rushing touchdowns. He had one game of 250 yards and 11 over 100. In 1975, he came close to matching his '73 season with 1,817 yards and 16 rushing touchdowns.

After nine seasons in Buffalo, O. J. finished his career with two seasons for the San Francisco 49ers. His career rushing totals were 2,404 attempts, 11,236 yards, and 61 rushing TDs. Simpson was named to the Pro Football Hall of Fame in 1985.

BRUCE SMITH

Few players will ever dominate a position the way Bruce Smith has mastered the defensive end spot for the Buffalo Bills. His speed and strength have made him one of the most feared and respected players in the modern game. Teams routinely double- if not triple-team the former Outland Trophy winner and Virginia Tech All-American. And, even though he's lightning quick, Smith is not just an outside pass rusher. "He's so powerful," Minnesota Vikings quarterback Warren Moon pointed out, "that he can bulldoze over you."

The first player selected in the 1985 NFL draft, Smith (born 1963) has been the Bills' prime defensive weapon since his rookie season. Named AFC Rookie of the Year by the NFL Players Association, he is Buffalo's all-time sack leader. A nine-time Pro Bowler, the 6′4″, 273-pounder has been named the AFC Defensive Player of the Year five times.

Most observers agree that the 1990 season was Smith's finest. His 19 quarterback sacks were second in the league, and more than once his dominant play changed the complexion of a game. Against the New York Jets, he recorded two sacks, defensed a pass, and forced two fumbles. In Week 14, against the Indianapolis Colts, he sacked quarterback Jeff George four times in the first 20 minutes of the game. And in Super Bowl XXV, he came up with one of the biggest plays of the game when he sacked New York Giants quarterback Jeff Hostetler in the end zone for a safety, giving the Bills a 12–3 lead.

Even after 12 seasons, Smith remained dedicated to preparing for an opponent. At 34, he showed no signs of slowing down and still spent countless hours studying game films and working out in the weight room. An intense player, Smith will eventually have to shift his focus from game-day preparation to the easier task of preparing for his inevitable induction into the Pro Football Hall of Fame.

BELOW: SMITH'S EXUBERANCE REVS UP *the Buffalo crowd, adding a "12th man" to the Bills' defense.* **OPPOSITE PAGE:** *In 1990, Smith had 19 regular-season sacks, only three short of the official NFL record.*

EMMITT SMITH

Emmitt J. Smith III has excelled at football at every level. He was a consensus All-America running back and prep Player of the Year by *Parade* and *USA Today* as a senior at Escambia (Florida) High School. At the University of Florida, where he was an All-American and three-time All-SEC selection, he established 58 school records in three seasons, including a career rushing mark of 3,928 yards.

Since joining the Dallas Cowboys as their No. 1 pick in 1990, Smith (born 1969) has been even more sensational. Almost immediately, he emerged as one of the game's greatest performers. Though not exceptionally fast, Smith combined quick moves with the power of a fullback. No one was more determined to reach the end zone.

A Pro Bowl choice in each of his first six seasons, he's the only player in NFL history to rush for more than 1,400 yards in five consecutive seasons. In 1995, he added to his ever-growing list of accomplishments when he set a new NFL mark for touchdowns scored in a season, with 25. At the same time, he compiled a career-best 1,773 yards rushing. Hardly one-dimensional, his 62 receptions in 1995 marked the fourth straight season in which the versatile running back caught 50 or more passes.

BELOW: IN THE 1995 SEASON OPENER *against the Giants, Smith scored four touchdowns, including one on a 60-yard burst. He scored 25 TDs that year to set an NFL record.* **OPPOSITE PAGE:** *San Francisco found the secret of defensing Smith in the 1994 NFL championship game; the 49ers scored 21 quick points in the opening minutes. Smith still scored two touchdowns, but the 49ers hung on to win 38–28.*

How valuable is Smith to the Dallas offense? Well, while football is more than a one-man sport, the Cowboys through 1995 were 62–8 in games where Emmitt had 20 or more carries and 43–5 in games where he gained at least 100 yards rushing. His 20 postseason touchdowns are an NFL record.

Already compared to the likes of Hall of Famers Walter Payton and Jim Brown, Smith uses the comparisons as motivation. "When my career's over," he said, "I want to be able to say. . .no, I want to have the new kids, the new backs, say, 'Boy, we have to chase a legend to be the best,' and they'll mean Emmitt Smith."

AMOS ALONZO STAGG

ith the possible exception of Walter Camp, Amos Alonzo Stagg was the most important figure in the development of football into a great national game. And even though Camp was responsible for the rules that changed football from a rugby-soccer derivative into a uniquely American sport, Stagg—in his long career as player, coach, innovator, spokesman, and conscience of the game—may have done more to popularize it.

Stagg (1862–1965) first achieved prominence as a baseball player at Yale, pitching the Elis to perennial Big Three (Yale, Harvard, and Princeton) championships. As a football player, he was named an end on the first All-America team in 1889. He turned down a baseball contract offered by the New York Giants to enter Yale Divinity School, but believing he was a poor public speaker, he entered the YMCA Training School at Springfield, Massachusetts. He coached the Springfield football team and also took part in the first basketball game, aiding Dr. James Naismith in that sport's creation.

In 1892, Stagg became football coach at the University of Chicago, where he remained until mandatory retirement at age 70 forced him to leave in 1932. His Chicago teams, though nearly always outmanned, won seven Western Conference titles and had four undefeated seasons. Much of his success stemmed from his hundreds of innovations—everything from the invention of the tackling dummy to the Statue of Liberty play. He also served on the NCAA Rules Committee. Painfully honest, his unquestioned integrity made him the leading spokesman for college football during this period.

After leaving Chicago, Stagg became head coach at College of Pacific. In 1943, at age 81, he was voted national Coach of the Year when little COP registered seven wins over major teams. He resigned after the 1946 season but continued as an assistant for 12 more years, first at Susquehanna University under one of his sons and finally at Stockton J.C. In 57 years as a head coach, he compiled a record of 314–199–35.

BELOW: STAGG WAS TWICE ENSHRINED *in the National Football Foundation's College Hall of Fame, as a player and as a coach. He was also elected to the National Basketball Hall of Fame for his early contributions to that sport.* **OPPOSITE PAGE:** *The nearly 70-year-old Stagg shows members of his final University of Chicago team the proper way to hold for a place kick. Don Birney makes the boot.*

ROGER STAUBACH

center. He also helped popularize the Cowboys' "shotgun" offense. **OPPOSITE PAGE:** *Staubach launches another last-ditch comeback. During his 11 seasons with Dallas, he won 14 games in the last two minutes or in overtime.*

Roger Staubach earned the 1963 Heisman Trophy as an All-America quarterback at Navy while leading the Midshipmen to second place in the national rankings. The Dallas Cowboys made him a 10th-round draft choice in 1964 even though they knew they'd have to wait four years while he finished his obligation to the service before he could play pro football. When he finally showed up in the Cowboys' training camp in 1969, Staubach (born 1942) was a 27-year-old rookie carrying more rust than any ship he'd ever served on.

For two seasons, Staubach backed incumbent Craig Morton. When he finally became No. 1 in 1971, Roger made the most of it, winning the NFL passing championship, being named Player of the Year, and leading the Cowboys to victory over Miami in Super Bowl VI.

Staubach's 1972 season was all but wiped out by injury, but he came back stronger than ever in 1973. His nickname of "Captain Comeback" might well have applied to his own ability to bounce back from adversity, but in fact it referred to his remarkable knack for bringing his team back to victory from the brink of defeat. No fewer than 23 times did he lead the Cowboys to fourth-quarter comebacks. On 14 of those occasions, the winning points came in the final two minutes or in overtime.

His most famous comeback came in a 1975 playoff game against the Vikings. With the Cowboys trailing 14–10 and only 24 seconds to go, he lined up at the 50-yard line. Under a heavy rush by Minnesota, Staubach cut loose with a high, arching pass that receiver Drew Pearson somehow grabbed near the goal line for the victory. The pass became known as the original "Hail Mary."

From 1973–79, the 6'3", 202-pound Staubach won three more passing titles, took Dallas to three more NFC championships, and led his team to a win in Super Bowl XII. His career passing stats were 2,958 attempts, 1,685 completions, 22,700 yards, and 153 touchdowns. He also ran for 2,264 yards and a 5.5 average, earning himself another nickname—"Roger the Dodger."

JIM TAYLOR

I t was the worst of times and the best of times for Jim Taylor. Worst because in eras other than the one that featured Jim Brown, Taylor might have been considered pro football's premier fullback. Best because he was able to star for the winningest team of the time, the Green Bay Packers of Vince Lombardi.

Even though he was overshadowed by Brown in most seasons, Taylor (born 1935) carved out an enviable reputation as a man who could get crucial yards. Lombardi called him "the most determined runner I've ever seen." His five straight seasons of gaining more than 1,000 yards was something even Brown never accomplished.

An All-American at Louisiana State in 1957, Taylor was used only sparingly when he joined the Packers, even though the team was at the very bottom of the NFL standings. Only in the Packers' last two games was he given the football. When coach Lombardi took over the team in 1959, he studied films of all the Packers games of the year before and discovered his fullback.

Taylor absorbed Lombardi's "run to daylight" philosophy and blossomed into a great runner. Though undersized for a fullback at 215 pounds, Taylor was a weight-lifting addict and able to generate astonishing blasting power when he lowered his head and slammed into defenders. He led the Packers in rushing each year from 1960–66, a period in which Green Bay won five division titles and four NFL championships, including their victory in Super Bowl I.

TAYLOR ATTRIBUTED HIS ACCOMPLISH- *ments less to talent than to desire. His belief was that the player who wanted success the most would usually achieve it.*

Taylor's greatest season was 1962, when his 1,474 rushing yards topped all NFL runners including Jim Brown. He also led the NFL in scoring with 114 points on 19 touchdowns. A fierce blocker whether protecting Packer quarterback Bart Starr or leading halfback Paul Hornung on the famous "Packer Sweep," Taylor gained most of his own yardage between the tackles. Taylor, who was named to the Pro Football Hall of Fame in 1976, rushed for 8,597 yards and 83 touchdowns in 10 NFL seasons.

TAYLOR WAS FRUSTRATED IN THE 1960 *championship game when the Eagles' Chuck Bednarik tackled him on the way to a winning touchdown and then held him down until time ran out. This 49–0 Green Bay win over Philadelphia in 1962 was partial payback.*

LAWRENCE TAYLOR

"**I**f there was ever a Superman in the NFL," said former Washington Redskins quarterback Joe Theismann, "I think he wore No. 56 for the Giants." Although it's high praise to be compared to the fictitious Man of Steel, in Lawrence Taylor's case it's entirely appropriate.

When Taylor (born 1959) arrived in New York in 1981, the Giants hadn't been to the playoffs in 17 seasons. They hadn't even had a winning record for eight years. So the rookie first-round pick out of the University of North Carolina made it his personal quest to return his new team to greatness. Starting in Taylor's first season, the Giants began a 10-season streak in which they made the playoffs six times and won two Super Bowls. "He was the catalyst," said Bill Parcells, his former coach.

The consummate player, Taylor redefined the linebacker position. He had the speed to run past offensive linemen and the strength to outmuscle them. During 13 seasons with the Giants, he recorded 132½ quarterback sacks, 1,088 tackles, 33 forced fumbles, 10 fumble recoveries, and nine interceptions.

Part of his greatness was his ability to affect the outcome of a game. Such was the case in a meeting against the New Orleans Saints in 1988. In that game, the Giants played without quarterback Phil Simms and linebacker Carl Banks, who were nursing injuries. Taylor, who was suffering with a torn pectoral muscle in his shoulder, should have joined them on the sidelines. Wearing a harness to keep his shoulder in place, he managed to record an incredible seven tackles, three sacks, and two forced fumbles. The Giants won a squeaker 13–12. "I thought that was his most spectacular game," declared Parcells. "I thought it was his finest hour from a courage standpoint."

Taylor's accomplishments are many. A 10-time Pro Bowl selection, he recorded a career-high 20½ sacks and was named the NFL's MVP in 1986. In 1994, L. T. moved one step closer to his eventual Hall of Fame enshrinement when he was named to the NFL's 75th Anniversary All-Time Team.

ABOVE: WHEN TAYLOR RETIRED AFTER *the 1993 season, the Giants retired his number. He becomes eligible for the Pro Football Hall of Fame in 1999.*
OPPOSITE PAGE: *Taylor's ability to dominate a game with his attack style changed the outside linebacker position from a read-and-react posture to an aggressive mode. Here, Washington's Jay Schroeder learns the hard way.*

JIM THORPE

When Jim Thorpe won both the decathlon and pentathlon in the 1912 Olympics at Stockholm, Sweden's King Gustav proclaimed the obvious: "You, sir, are the greatest athlete in the world." Thorpe replied, "Thanks, King."

Of mixed Irish, Sauk, and Fox ancestry, Thorpe (1888–1953) was born in what is now Oklahoma, but when he was 16 his father sent him east to Carlisle Institute in Pennsylvania, the famous school for Indian youth. There, under legendary coach Glenn "Pop" Warner, he first achieved football fame in 1908 with a pair of long touchdown runs in Carlisle's tie with powerful Penn. But Thorpe was an indifferent student. He dropped out of school in 1909 and, among other things, played some semipro baseball.

Lured back to Carlisle in 1911 by Warner, Thorpe became a two-year All-American and experienced his Olympic triumphs. But shortly after the 1912 football season, knowledge of Thorpe's baseball days surfaced. He was declared a professional, and the Olympic Committee demanded he return his medals. (They were restored to his family in 1982.)

Although he played six seasons of major-league baseball, football was Thorpe's game. In 1915, the Canton Bulldogs offered him $250 a game at a time when few stars could command even $100. With Thorpe as star and coach, the Bulldogs won the U.S. professional championship in 1916, '17, and '19. His presence moved pro football a giant step forward in the public's estimation.

Thorpe could do everything: plunge through lines, outrace pursuers, and throw and catch passes. He was an outstanding punter and such a deadly kicker that he gave pregame exhibitions—place-kicking field goals from the 50-yard line, then turning and drop-kicking through the opposite goal posts. He was such a punishing tackler that opponents accused him of wearing sheet metal in his shoulder pads.

When the NFL was formed in 1920, Thorpe was named its first president, though more for his name than his executive ability.

THORPE STILL GETS VOTES AS THE *greatest athlete of the 20th century. Who else was an Olympic champion, a major-league baseball player, and an All-American and All-Pro in football?*

THORPE WAS PROBABLY THE BEST *all-around kicker of his time. Punt, place kick, or drop kick, he could do it all.*

Y. A. TITTLE

In an age when quarterbacks are too often judged by how many Super Bowl rings cluster their fingers, Yelberton Abraham Tittle gained enshrinement in the Pro Football Hall of Fame despite never winning an NFL championship. The voters knew he was a winner even if that could not always be said about the teams he directed.

After a fine career at Louisiana State, Tittle (born 1926) spent his first three pro seasons (1948–50) with the Baltimore Colts. Although his personal statistics were impressive, the Colts were corralled at the bottom of the AAFC and, in their final year (before their rebirth in 1953), proved an embarrassment to the NFL. Tittle wound up with the San Francisco 49ers—a giant step up from the Colts—but also a team stocked with stars and holes, always promising but never quite delivering.

Nicknamed "Colonel Slick" for his clever ball-handling and sharp play-calling, Tittle was said to be the league's best long passer, yet he had "touch" for short passing and a streak of originality. He and receiver R. C. Owens invented and perfected the "alley-oop"—a rainbow spiral that dropped from the clouds just as the leaping Owens rose like a rocket to cradle it.

In 1961, the 49ers decided "Yat" was near the end of his road and dealt him to the New York Giants. There, he embarked on his greatest seasons. First, he had to beat out his friend Chuck Conerly, the Giants' quarterback since 1948. Tittle not only won the starting job but took the Giants to the Eastern Division title. His 2,272 passing yards and 17 touchdown passes earned him league MVP consideration.

Two more Eastern crowns followed as Tittle's TD passes rose to record heights—33 in 1962 and 36 in 1963, when he was voted the league's Player of the Year. Though Tittle's Giants lost three straight championship games, each was to a great team—two to the Packers of Vince Lombardi and the third to the defensively dominant Bears of 1963.

BELOW: Tittle was the quarterback *of an amazing San Francisco backfield in the mid-1950s. He and runners Hugh McElhenny, Joe Perry, and John Henry Johnson all were eventually enshrined in the Pro Football Hall of Fame.*
Opposite page: *Tittle led the Giants to three straight championship games from 1961–63—all losses. In the 1963 loss to the Bears, a first-half leg injury kept him from throwing naturally, causing five interceptions.*

EMLEN TUNNELL

ABOVE: THE NFL DRAFT BEGAN IN *1936. Tunnell was the first undrafted free agent to be elected to the Pro Football Hall of Fame. Others are Night Train Lane, Willie Wood, Willie Brown, Larry Little, and Jim Langer.* **OPPOSITE PAGE:** *Tunnell eludes Cleveland's Ken Gorgal (left) and Jim Martin in a 1950 game. The Browns lost just two games all year, both to Tunnell's Giants.*

Sometimes good fortune arrives unexpectedly. Certainly the New York Giants had no inkling it had come their way when Emlen Tunnell walked into their offices in 1948 and asked for a tryout. Probably no Giants staff member had even heard of the 6'1", 200-pound halfback who had sat out his senior season at Iowa because of eye surgery.

Tunnell (1925–1975) got his tryout, made the team, and quickly came to be regarded as New York's best defensive back and a superior kick returner. The NFL's merger with the AAFC in 1950 brought the Giants three more outstanding defensive backs in Tom Landry, Otto Schnellbacher, and Harmon Rowe. Those three and Tunnell formed the pass-protecting "ribs" of the Giants' famed "Umbrella Defense," which revolutionized defensive thinking in the early 1950s.

"Emlen the Gremlin" was the most honored of the quartet. He was named All-NFL four times and played in nine Pro Bowls. Not only was he a pass-snatching ball-hawk, but he paralyzed opponents with his brilliant returns of interceptions, kick-offs, and punts. He was called "The Giants' Offense on Defense" for good reason. In 1952, his return yardage was greater than that achieved by any New York ball carrier or pass receiver. In fact, it was more than the yardage gained by NFL rushing leader Dan Towler.

While the other ribs of the umbrella retired or, like Landry, became more deeply involved in coaching, Tunnell continued to excel at safety as the Giants won the NFL championship in 1956 and a division title in 1958. In 1959, he went to Green Bay and helped Vince Lombardi turn that teetering franchise into a dynasty. When he retired after the 1961 season, Tunnell held the NFL career records for interceptions (79), interception yardage (1,282), punt returns (258), and punt return yardage (2,209).

When he was elected to the Pro Football Hall of Fame in 1967, he was both the first African American to be enshrined and the first player to be named for strictly his defensive contributions.

JOHNNY UNITAS

J ohnny Unitas was cut by the Pittsburgh Steelers before he even got a chance to throw one pass in a preseason game. The Steelers' ninth-round draft pick from the University of Louisville then played semipro football with the Bloomfield (Pennsylvania) Rams for $6 per game when Baltimore Colts coach Weeb Ewbank decided to take a chance on the kid with the crewcut. He signed him to a $7,000 contract.

Unitas (born 1933) got his second break when injury sidelined Colts starting quarterback George Shaw in the fourth game of the 1956 season. Hoping to make the most of his opportunity, "Johnny U" got off to a rocky start when his first pass as a pro was intercepted. A lesser man might have hung his head and quit, but not Unitas. He finished the game with his head held high, and within just a few seasons he was being hailed as pro football's "living legend."

Unitas, the NFL's three-time Most Valuable Player, accumulated almost unbelievable statistics during his 18-year career with the Colts (1956–72) and San Diego Chargers (1973). When he retired, he held virtually every meaningful career passing record, including attempts (5,186), completions (2,830), yards (40,239), most 300-yard passing games (26), touchdown passes (290), and most consecutive games throwing a touchdown pass (47).

But without a doubt, it's for his heroic performance in the 1958 NFL title game, often referred to as the "Greatest Game Ever Played," that he is best remembered. His tying and winning drives were textbook-perfect examples of what it takes to win under pressure. Late in the game, with the Colts trailing the New York Giants 17–14, Unitas completed seven straight passes. That set up the game's tying field goal with just seven seconds left. He followed that All-Pro performance with a perfectly executed 80-yard touchdown drive in overtime to win.

In 1979, with his election to the Pro Football Hall of Fame, Johnny Unitas completed his climb to the top, proving that sometimes all that is needed is a chance to play.

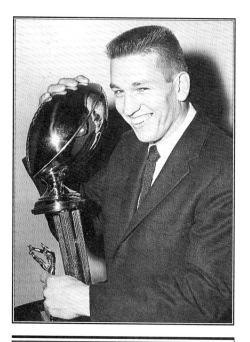

ABOVE: TWO DAYS BEFORE CHRISTMAS in 1957, the "quarterback Pittsburgh cut" collected the Jim Thorpe Trophy as the Newspaper Enterprise Association's choice as league MVP. **OPPOSITE PAGE:** Unitas passed for 361 yards—and ran for 26—in Baltimore's fabled victory in the 1958 NFL championship game. Note that Unitas is the only player wearing high-tops.

GENE UPSHAW

Gene Upshaw was the first modern-era player who performed exclusively as a guard to be elected to the Pro Football Hall of Fame. It was an honor that would have seemed highly unlikely in his early years, since he didn't even play football until his senior year in high school.

Although Upshaw (born 1945) won a scholarship to Texas A&I College, it came only after he got a tryout as a walk-on. There, the 6'5", 255-pound Upshaw sparkled. He played center, tackle, and end and earned NAIA All-America honors as a senior.

The Oakland Raiders selected Gene in the first round of the 1967 draft. Raiders managing general partner Al Davis had already envisioned Upshaw as the guard who could contain the big defensive tackles like Buck Buchanan of the Raiders' arch rival, the Kansas City Chiefs. "I figured if Buchanan was going to play for the Chiefs for the next 10 years, we better get some big guy who could handle him," Davis said. "Those two guys put on some stirring battles over the years."

Over the next 15 seasons, Upshaw, who would miss just one game due to injury, was an integral part of a team that would play in three American Football League and seven American Football Conference championship games as well as three Super Bowls. During his first 14 seasons, the Raiders won an incredible 75 percent of their games, with a 148–47–7 regular-season record. An extremely effective lead blocker on wide running plays, Gene spearheaded the offensive line that made the Raiders' rushing attack the most feared in the league during the 1970s. "That's my play," he justifiably bragged. "That's where I get my satisfaction in football."

A team leader, Upshaw was the Raiders' offensive captain for eight years, was an All-AFL or All-AFC choice eight times, and played in six straight AFC/NFC Pro Bowls as well as the 1968 AFL All-Star Game. He became head of the NFL Players Association in 1987.

BELOW: BEFORE UPSHAW, OFFENSIVE *guards were usually stocky. The Raiders star used his height to combat defensive tackles, who had been overpowering shorter guards.* **OPPOSITE PAGE:** *Upshaw (#63) and fellow guard Wayne Hawkins pave the way for Raiders halfback Pete Banaszak in a 1967 meeting with arch rival Kansas City.*

NORM VAN BROCKLIN

THE "DUTCHMAN" COULD DO EVERY-
thing on a football field but run. Slow of foot, he became a classic pocket passer, a preference that caused friction when he later coached scrambler Fran Tarkenton.

Norm Van Brocklin's crowning achievement was the Philadelphia Eagles' 1960 NFL championship. The Eagles were definitely not the most talented team in the league that year, but Van Brocklin's passing—and, more important, his determined leadership—brought them victory. A month after the Eagles defeated the Packers for the title, Van Brocklin retired to become coach of the expansion Minnesota Vikings, writing *finis* to a stormy 12-season playing career.

In 1949, Van Brocklin (1926–1983) joined the Los Angeles Rams, opting to forego his final year of eligibility at the University of Oregon. The 6′1″, 190-pound sharpshooter was a firebrand leader, a fine field general, a brilliant passer, an exceptional punter, and perhaps the worst runner ever to get knocked flat in an NFL backfield. For that reason, he was a classic stay-in-the-pocket quarterback.

Although the "Dutchman" was ready for the Rams, the Rams already had a Hall of Fame-bound quarterback in Bob Waterfield. Van Brocklin and Waterfield shared playing time for four seasons until Waterfield retired. Van Brocklin led the NFL in passing in 1950 and 1952, and Waterfield led in 1951, the year the Rams won the NFL championship. In one game in '51, the Dutchman passed for an NFL-record 554 yards against the New York Yanks.

Despite both team and personal success, the super-competitive Van Brocklin chafed at sharing time at quarterback. Once Waterfield was out of the picture, the situation didn't improve much. Even though Norm won his third passing title in 1954 when he averaged over 10 yards per attempt, he still often found himself sharing time with another quarterback; young Bill Wade was the new phenom. Finally, Van Brocklin demanded a trade.

In 1958, the Rams exiled Van Brocklin to Philadelphia, a team habitually at the bottom of the standings. New Eagles coach Lawrence "Buck" Shaw gave Norm a virtual free hand with the offense, and the team improved each year, culminating in the 1960 championship season. In 12 seasons, Van Brocklin passed for 23,611 yards and 173 touchdowns. He also punted 523 times for a 42.9 average and "ran" (if you would call it that) for 11 scores.

THE LOS ANGELES RAMS FACED THE *Cleveland Browns in three NFL championship games. L.A. won in 1951 when Van Brocklin's 73-yard TD pass to Tom Fears provided the winning points.*

STEVE VAN BUREN

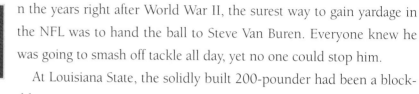

BELOW: SMALL AS A HIGH SCHOOL *player, Van Buren gained 35 pounds before entering LSU by working all summer in a steel mill.* **OPPOSITE PAGE:** *Packer Bruce Smith holds on for dear life in the Eagles' last regular-season game of 1947. Smith couldn't keep Van Buren from becoming only the second NFL player to run for 1,000 yards.*

I n the years right after World War II, the surest way to gain yardage in the NFL was to hand the ball to Steve Van Buren. Everyone knew he was going to smash off tackle all day, yet no one could stop him.

At Louisiana State, the solidly built 200-pounder had been a blocking back until his senior year, paving the way for star Alvin Dark, who went on to baseball fame. When Van Buren (born 1920) ran for over 800 yards in his final season with the Tigers, Philadelphia made him its first pick in the 1944 draft. He broke in with a bang, leading the league in punt returns and rushing for 444 yards. The following year, he led the NFL in rushing and kickoff returns. In a 10-game season, he scored 18 touchdowns—nearly two per game. Nevertheless, some regarded him as a "wartime wonder" who would fade once the "real" stars returned. Rather than fade, he got better.

Van Buren was a 9.8 sprinter in the 100-yard dash and surprisingly shifty in an open field. But he was foremost a power runner—the kind it hurt to tackle. He never seemed to tire. By the fourth quarter, he still slammed into opponents just as hard as he had in the first quarter.

The Eagles' success was tied to Van Buren. In 1947, he led them to their first division championship as he became only the second NFL runner to rush for over a 1,000 yards by gaining 1,008. He easily could have had a second 1,000-yard season in 1948 when he gained 945 yards, but he sat out a game against a weak Boston club to save himself for the championship game.

In that famous title tilt, played in a blizzard, he scored the only touchdown on a fourth-quarter smash. Van Buren took the Eagles to another league championship in 1949 while setting a new rushing record with 1,146 yards. In the championship game, he rumbled for 196 yards. He retired with the then-NFL record of 5,860 rushing yards.

DOAK WALKER

drafted by the since-defunct New York Bulldogs. He wound up in Detroit with high school pal Bobby Lane, whom the Lions also acquired from the Bulldogs. OPPOSITE PAGE: Walker soars for extra yardage against the Pittsburgh Steelers in 1953. Although small, Walker was adept at squirming through tiny holes in the line.

Doak Walker was one of the greatest college players ever. The Southern Methodist University triple threat was named All-American each year from 1947–49 and won the 1948 Heisman Trophy.

As a sophomore tailback in 1947, Walker (born 1927) ran, passed, and kicked the Mustangs to an undefeated season. His 38.7-yard kickoff return average set an NCAA record. After his Heisman-winning junior season, his face could be found on nearly every preseason football magazine. Readers who delved inside could learn that Doak was his middle name (his first name was Ewell) and that he was expected to be even better as a senior.

Injuries held Walker back much of his final college season, though he was deservedly named to most All-America teams. However, when it seemed he might again receive strong Heisman support, the modest star asked the committee to withdraw his name from consideration so that a player who'd been able to participate in all of his team's games might win.

Nevertheless, there were doubts that Walker could make it in the pros when he signed with the Detroit Lions. At 5'11" and 173 pounds, he was small and not enough of a "specialist" in any phase of his game. He ended up specializing in everything! During his six pro seasons, Walker ran for a 4.9 average, caught 152 passes, kicked 183 extra points and 49 field goals, threw halfback passes, ran back kicks, punted a few times, and—in a pinch—played defense.

Walker led the NFL in scoring twice, in his first year with 128 points and in his final season. He was named All-NFL four times and selected for five Pro Bowls. With "The Doaker" at halfback, Detroit won three division titles and two NFL championships. No doubt his signature play was his 67-yard dash off right tackle for the decisive touchdown against Cleveland in the 1952 championship game. Walker's election to the Pro Football Hall of Fame in 1986 gave him enshrinement in both the college and pro halls.

BILL WALSH

he traffic leading to Pontiac, Michigan's Silverdome and Super Bowl XVI was bumper-to-bumper, as thousands braved the frigid, icy conditions. Caught in the traffic melee was a bus carrying half of the San Francisco 49ers squad. Head coach Bill Walsh, sensing the heightened tensions of those on board, decided to speak. "Gentlemen," he began, "I've got good news and bad news. The bad news is that the game has begun without us. The good news is we're ahead 3–0." Laughter erupted.

ABOVE: THE PROFESSOR EXPLAINS A FINE *point of strategy to his prize pupil, Joe Montana. Behind these two masterminds, San Francisco perennially led the NFC in total offense.* **OPPOSITE PAGE:** *Walsh is carried off the field after the 49ers' 38–16 victory over the Miami Dolphins in Super Bowl XIX.*

Walsh (born 1931) was a masterful leader. Be it with a tension-breaking corny joke or a risky play call, he knew it was his job to recognize and react to the needs of his team. For 10 seasons with the 49ers (1979–88), he did just that. In the process, he took a team that in 1978 was the NFL's worst and turned it into a Super Bowl champion in just three seasons. Under Walsh, the 49ers achieved a level of success they'd never before reached, winning three Super Bowls (in January 1982, '85, and '89) and capturing six NFC West titles.

Walsh built his winning teams with the careful selection of talented players. He selected future stars Joe Montana and Dwight Clark in his first draft as 49ers coach. He added Ronnie Lott and Eric Wright in 1981, added Roger Craig in 1983, and in 1985 traded up to select Jerry Rice. Never did he allow himself to become complacent or stop trying to improve his team. As a result, only seven players appeared in each of the 49ers' three Super Bowls victories.

Walsh's 102–63–1 record is the best ever for a 49ers coach. Most agree that his finest coaching performance came in 1987, when in a two-week period injuries forced him to make seven changes on offense, including five to the offensive line. Injuries also necessitated changes on the defensive line and in the linebacking corps. Still, the Hall of Fame coach managed to advance his team to postseason play for a fifth consecutive year.

PAUL WARFIELD

Paul Warfield is recognized as one of the premier wide receivers ever to have played in the NFL. His career totals for number of catches don't seem to be in line with those accumulated by other great receivers. However, as any student of the game should understand, the truth isn't always in the numbers.

During his 14 seasons with the Cleveland Browns (1964–69, 1976–77), the Miami Dolphins (1970–74), and the Memphis Grizzlies (1975) of the World Football League, the former Ohio State star played on ball-control teams. Even so, Warfield (born 1942) managed to haul in 452 career receptions for 8,987 yards and 88 touchdowns. His 19.88 yards-per-catch mark still ranks as one of the best in the history of the game.

Because of his blazing speed, elusive moves, and great leaping ability, defenses more often than not found it necessary to double-team Warfield. A long-ball threat, he intimidated the opposition. His mere presence on the football field proved to be almost as beneficial to the running game as it was to the passing game. The best example of this may have been in 1972 when the Dolphins posted their remarkable 17–0 season. During that campaign, Miami ran the ball 613 times while passing on just 259 occasions. Their philosophy was to use the forward pass as a threat to make the ground attack more effective. The Dolphins rushed for a then-NFL-record 2,960 yards.

As a rookie with the Browns, Warfield caught a career-high 52 passes. His outside speed was the perfect complement to the power running of fullback Jim Brown. Together, they led the Browns to their first NFL title in nine years. During Warfield's first six years with the Browns, the team posted an impressive 59–23–2 record and played in five conference championships, as well as the 1964 championship game.

BELOW: WARFIELD HAULS IN A *touchdown pass on the first play of the game against the Lions in 1973. Before the quarter ended, Warfield scored again.* **OPPOSITE PAGE:** *Warfield, shown here about to grab a pass against the Cowboys, combined speed, sure hands, and exceptional grace to make him a threat on every play.*

POP WARNER

ABOVE: WARNER LOOKS OUT ACROSS *the field at his 1932 Stanford team, hoping to find another Jim Thorpe or Ernie Nevers. Warner resigned from Stanford after the season after alumni grumbled about his five straight losses to Southern Cal.* **OPPOSITE PAGE:** *Warner prepares his Temple squad in 1936, two years after he took the Owls to the first Sugar Bowl.*

During the 1920s and 1930s, the two most famous and respected football coaches in the nation were Knute Rockne and Glenn "Pop" Warner. Despite their success, the two were complete opposites. Rockne was extroverted, inspirational—a motivator who radiated warmth. Warner was cerebral, inventive—a tactician described as "gruff, sometimes almost surly and sullen." Despite Rockne's charisma, an Associated Press poll in the 1950s named Warner as the greatest coach of all time.

Warner (1871–1954) gained his nickname of "Pop" when he arrived at Cornell University as a 21-year-old freshman. When he graduated with a law degree in 1895, he thought he had finished with sports. Then coaching offers arrived. That fall, he left for the University of Georgia to begin a coaching career that spanned 44 years.

In 1897, Warner returned to Cornell to coach. A one-sided victory over the Carlisle Indians in 1898 caused Carlisle to offer him the position of coach and athletic director. There he first gained national attention. The little government school played the strongest college teams and often won on speed and superior coaching. Warner's most famous player was, of course, Jim Thorpe.

When Carlisle began phasing out its football program, Warner accepted an offer to coach the University of Pittsburgh. His first three Pittsburgh teams went undefeated and won or shared the national title. In 1924, he moved to Stanford University, where he developed fullback Ernie Nevers, a player he regarded as even better than Thorpe because "he always tried harder." Warner's Stanford teams went to three Rose Bowls, and the 1926 squad was ranked No. 1 in the country.

Warner was one of the most innovative coaches in history—so creative that he is sometimes considered the inventor of things that he may have only developed. Certainly he was the creator of the single- and double-wing formations, football's dominant offensive sets for more than 30 years. By one count, he produced 47 All-Americans. His final record was 313–106–32, placing him near the top of any list of great coaches.

BOB WATERFIELD

ob Waterfield burst onto the pro football scene in 1945, when he quarterbacked the Cleveland Rams to the NFL championship, sealing the crown with a pair of touchdown passes in the title game. He was named both Rookie of the Year and Most Valuable Player.

The following season, the Rams moved to Los Angeles, and Bob went home. He had starred at UCLA, where he met and eventually wed movie queen Jane Russell. As Ram QB—later splitting time with Norm Van Brocklin—Waterfield (1920–1983) took the team to three straight title games, 1949–51. The Rams won it all in '51 with a 24–17 win over the Cleveland Browns in the title game. For all his athletic ability, Waterfield's quiet and unemotional leadership was equally important to his team's success. In the 1950 divisional playoff, the 6′2″, 200-pound Waterfield was unable to practice all week because of the flu, but he came off the bench to throw three touchdown passes in a 24–14 win over the Bears.

As a passer, Waterfield was known for his ability to throw deep. He led the NFL in passing in 1946 and 1951, finishing with career totals of 1,617 attempts for 814 completions, 11,849 yards gained, and 97 touchdown passes.

Bob was one of the most versatile players in NFL history. In addition to his QB chores, he was an ace defensive back for his first four years in the NFL, a top punter with a 42.4 average, and a deadly place-kicker. In eight seasons, he totaled 573 points on 13 TDs, 315 PATs, and 60 field goals. And, although running with the football wasn't part of his job description, he could do that effectively in a pinch. Some credit him with having invented the "bootleg" play.

In one 1948 game, the Rams fell behind eventual league champion Philadelphia 28–0. Waterfield rallied his team to a tie on four late touchdown passes. After the game, Rams coach Clark Shaughnessy could only rave about Waterfield's ability as a defensive back! He had held Eagle All-Pro end Pete Pihos without a reception. Waterfield was named to the Pro Football Hall of Fame in 1965.

REGGIE WHITE

n ordained Baptist minister, Reggie White's off-the-field humanitarian service to his community and church are well documented. However, on the field, that's another matter. No quarterback in the NFL would ever describe White's actions as "humanitarian."

Nicknamed the "Minister of Defense," White (born 1961) is the NFL's preeminent sack artist. He is the only NFL player to register double-digit sack totals in nine consecutive seasons (1985–93). His dominating play at defensive end for the Philadelphia Eagles (1985–92) and the Green Bay Packers (since 1993) earned him 11 consecutive Pro Bowl invitations, a record for a defensive end.

After an outstanding career at the University of Tennessee, White began his pro football career in 1984 with the Memphis Showboats of the United States Football League. Selected by the NFL's Eagles as their first-round choice in the supplemental draft of USFL players, he joined Philadelphia in the fourth week of the 1985 season. His NFL debut versus the New York Giants was nothing short of remarkable. The 6′5″, 300-pound terror recorded 2½ sacks and deflected a pass that was intercepted by a teammate and returned for a touchdown. In the strike-shortened 1987 season, he registered 21 sacks, just one short of the NFL record, despite appearing in just 12 games.

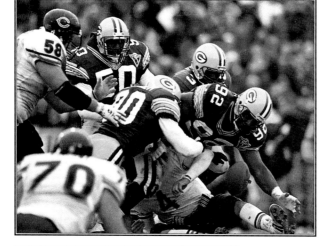

THE "MINISTER OF DEFENSE" PREACHES *a hard sermon, causing the Chicago Bears to repent their wicked ways.*

When it comes to durability, Reggie White wrote the book. In his first 12 NFL seasons, he missed just one game, that after tearing a hamstring in a December 10, 1995, game against the Tampa Bay Buccaneers. Thought to be lost for the season, White surprised everyone, including his doctors, when he suited up the following week for a pivotal game against the New Orleans Saints. Not only did White finish the regular season, but he played throughout the Packers' playoff run that fell one game short of a Super Bowl appearance. "It's just another situation where something miraculous happened to me again," White said, "and I thank God for it." One year later, White led the Pack to victory in Super Bowl XXXI.

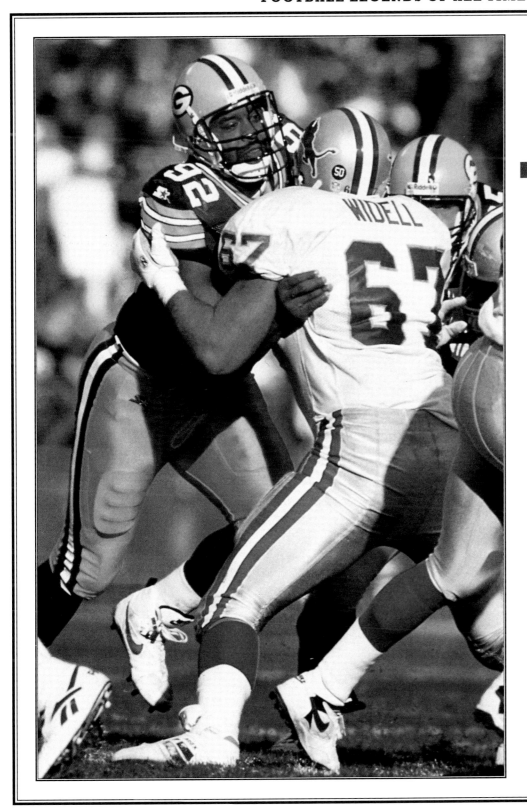

WHITE, SHOWN MANHANDLING

Detroit guard Doug Widell, signed with Green Bay to pursue his dream of a Super Bowl—a dream realized after the 1996 season.

BILL WILLIS

The cat-quick Bill Willis earned All-America honors at Ohio State as a two-way tackle on the national championship team of 1942 and the high-ranked '44 squad. But pro football seemed closed because of the NFL's unwritten ban on African-American players. A friend suggested he try out for the Cleveland Browns of the newly formed All-America Football Conference, scheduled to start play in the fall of 1946. The Browns were led by Paul Brown, who had coached Willis at Ohio State.

Willis (born 1921) showed up unannounced at the Browns' training camp. He earned a starting job in his first practice scrimmage by blasting past the team's NFL-experienced center to nab the quarterback again and again. A few days later, when fullback Marion Motley joined the team, the AAFC had its first two African Americans. Both went on to Hall of Fame careers.

Willis's power and quickness on defense brought him continuous all-league recognition. Because his sudden, explosive charge on the snap catapulted him into the enemy's backfield before a play could get started, frustrated opponents often insisted he was off-sides.

The Browns won four straight AAFC titles, with Willis a key performer first as both an offensive and defensive guard and, after two years, as a defensive specialist at middle guard. Although he anchored one of the most effective defenses in pro football, the 210-pound Willis was tiny for the middle guard position. "They listed me on the program at 225 pounds," Willis said. "It was a psychological thing. (Coach) Paul Brown didn't want the other teams to know I was really that small."

In 1950, Cleveland entered the NFL and continued its success with an NFL championship. Willis's game-saving tackle against the New York Giants keyed the playoff victory that put the Browns into the championship game. Besides annual All-Pro selections, the soft-spoken Willis was named to the first three Pro Bowls.

BELOW: WILLIS'S NO. 36 INDICATES *that this photo was taken while the Cleveland Browns were winning four straight All-America Football Conference championships.* **OPPOSITE PAGE:** *Willis continued his All-Pro play in the NFL, wearing No. 60. Here he uses his speed to chase the Giants' Chuck Conerly in 1952.*

LARRY WILSON

BELOW: WILSON WAVES TO AN *appreciative St. Louis crowd after his final game in 1972. Do those eyes look moist?* **OPPOSITE PAGE:** *Two Hall of Famers meet: Cleveland's Leroy Kelly uses a block-tackle to end Wilson's interception return during a rare Cardinals victory over the Browns in 1968.*

O n November 7, 1965, the St. Louis Cardinals defeated the Pittsburgh Steelers 21–17 to remain in contention for the league's Eastern Conference title. Cardinals safety Larry Wilson set the tone of the game when, early in the first quarter, he burst through the Steelers' offensive line and batted down a Bill Nelson pass. As the ball fell aimlessly toward the ground, Wilson scooped it out of mid-air and rambled 34 yards to the Pittsburgh 3. The Cardinals scored on the next play. While big plays were nothing new for the Cardinals' All-Pro safety, what made this one different was that Wilson was playing with casts on both hands, having a week earlier sustained a broken left hand and a broken finger on his right hand.

Wilson (born 1938) rightfully earned the reputation of being the "toughest player in the NFL." The Cardinals' innovative safety blitz was designed around the 6'0", 190-pound defensive back. "I had to wait for the right player to execute it," explained Chuck Drulis, the Cardinals' defensive coordinator and blitz architect. "He had to be quick, he had to be a hard tackler, and he had to have a lot of guts because he could be belted really hard by those big offensive linemen if anything went wrong. Larry had all those attributes."

A seventh-round draft choice out of Utah in 1960, Wilson had serious doubts that he would even make the Cardinals team. Not only did the future Hall of Famer make the team, but he started as a rookie and made the first of his eight Pro Bowl appearances in 1962. In addition to being a deadly effective blitzer, Wilson was also recognized as an outstanding coverage man. He led the league in interceptions in 1966 with 10, including a string of seven games in which he had at least one pick. He finished his career with a club-record 52 interceptions. According to Steelers Hall of Fame quarterback Bobby Layne, Wilson "may have been the toughest guy, pound-for-pound, who ever played this game."

KELLEN WINSLOW

T he 1981 AFC divisional playoff game between the San Diego Chargers and the Miami Dolphins was truly a game for the ages. The epic match ended with just 1:08 left in overtime when Rolf Benirschke kicked a 29-yard field goal to give the Chargers a 41–38 victory. The teams traded possession six times in the overtime period.

Most remember the game, however, for the courageous play of Chargers tight end Kellen Winslow. For much of the game, the 6′5″, 250-pound Winslow suffered dehydration from the heat and humidity and numbness in an injured shoulder. Three times he was helped off the field; each time he returned to catch yet another of his playoff-record 13 receptions. And if that wasn't enough, he even blocked what would have been a game-winning field goal with just seconds remaining in regulation play. It was vintage Winslow.

A gifted athlete, Winslow (born 1957) did not play high school football until his senior year because his mother feared he might get seriously injured. Even after just one season of high school football, he received offers from four schools— Kansas State, Kansas, Missouri, and Northwestern. He chose the University of Missouri, where he captured All-America honors. In four seasons, he caught 71 passes for 1,089 yards and 10 touchdowns.

Selected in the first round of the 1979 NFL draft, Winslow got off to a quick start with 25 receptions before being sidelined with a broken leg in the seventh game. He returned in 1980 with a career-high 89 receptions for 1,290 yards. Twice more he made 88 catches.

Even though he was plagued by injuries through much of his nine-year career, Winslow still amassed an impressive 541 receptions for 6,741 yards and 45 touchdowns. At the time of his retirement, he ranked 14th among all NFL pass receivers in number of receptions. It's fair to say that Kellen Winslow didn't merely play tight end, he redefined the position.

BELOW: WINSLOW GAVE QUARTERBACK *Dan Fouts a big target in San Diego's pass-happy "Air Coryell" offense.* **OPPOSITE PAGE:** *Because of his parents' fear of injuries, Winslow was allowed to compete in only one high school "sport"—chess. He was finally allowed to play football during his senior year.*

ROD WOODSON

in 1995. A knee injury he suffered in the Steelers' opening game apparently ended his season, but a brutal rehab program got him back in time to play in Super Bowl XXX. **OPPOSITE PAGE:** *Woodson, shown here on a return against the Oilers, has excelled at pass coverage. But what has really set him apart has been his hard tackling and surprise blitzes of rival quarterbacks.*

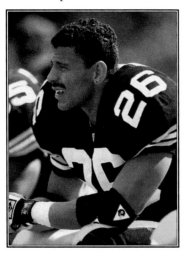

od Woodson did it all during his college career at Purdue. He played running back and wide receiver on offense, played cornerback and safety on defense, and returned punts and kickoffs. A consensus All-American, Woodson broke 13 Purdue records. In his final regular-season game in his senior year, he rushed for 93 yards, had three interceptions for 67 yards, returned two kickoffs for 46 yards and three punts for 30 yards, made 10 tackles, and forced a fumble.

Although Woodson (born 1965) envisioned himself as a "triple threat" player when the Pittsburgh Steelers made him their No. 1 pick in the 1987 draft, head coach Chuck Noll felt otherwise. Noll reasoned that his young star was too valuable to risk by playing both offense and defense. He wanted him to concentrate on returning kicks and playing cornerback. And his coach's discipline paid off when Woodson earned Pro Bowl honors as both a kick return specialist and a cornerback.

But it wasn't until Noll's successor, Bill Cowher, took over that Woodson really blossomed. In 1992, he led the Steelers in tackles and collected six sacks—a rare accomplishment for a cornerback. The following season, the "Man of Steel" had 28 passes defensed, knocked down another two at the line of scrimmage, forced two fumbles, had two quarterback sacks, blocked a field goal attempt, and recorded a team-high 79 solo tackles. For his efforts, he was named NFL Defensive Player of the Year.

There were more honors in 1994. The most impressive was being named to the NFL's 75th Anniversary All-Time Team—a distinction reserved for just five active players. But misfortune struck in the opening game of the 1995 season when the three-time team MVP suffered a knee injury that required reconstructive surgery. Recovery time was projected to be six to 12 months. But like another man of steel, the Steelers' Superman stunned the skeptics when he returned to action in just four months and played in Super Bowl XXX.

Front cover: **Richard Kane/SportsChrome USA.**